Faithful Inspiration

"And let the beauty of the Lord our God be upon us: and establish thou the work of our hands upon us; yea, the work of our hands establish thou it."

Psalm 90:17

What better way to celebrate your blessings or find comfort in your faith than to spend quiet moments stitching and meditating? This collection of richly detailed cross stitch designs offers you thirty-seven ways to recreate popular Christian images, poetry, and scripture. Is there someone who needs to hear that you love them? Stitch a heartfelt message for a special mother or daughter. Let a friend know how much you treasure her friendship, and remind those you cherish that comfort is never far away. Whatever your age and wherever you are in your journey, in this book you will find many special projects to create and share.

These classic designs are among our all-time favorites, and their timeless messages will appeal to believers of all ages. May the work of your hands bring lightness to your heart.

Deb

Deb Moore
Craft Publications Director

Leisure Arts, Inc.
Little Rock, Arkansas

EDITORIAL STAFF

Vice President and Editor-in-Chief:
Sandra Graham Case

Executive Publications Director:
Cheryl Nodine Gunnells

Senior Publications Director:
Susan White Sullivan

Designer Relations Director:
Debra Nettles

Craft Publications Director:
Deb Moore

Senior Prepress Director:
Mark Hawkins

Art Publications Director:
Rhonda Shelby

Art Category Manager:
Chaska Richardson Lucas

Contributing Creative Director:
Joel Tressler

Contributing Production Artist:
Charlie Thomas

Editorial Writer:
Susan McManus Johnson

Technical Writers:
Joyce Harris and Jane Prather

Photography Manager:
Katherine Atchison

Imaging Technicians: Brian Hall,
Stephanie Johnson, and Mark R. Potter

Publishing Systems Administrator:
Becky Riddle

Publishing Systems Assistants:
Clint Hanson, Brian Richardson,
and John Rose

Staff Photographer:
Lloyd Litsey

Photography Stylists:
Janna Laughlin and Christy Myers

Contributing Photographers:
Jerry Davis and Mark Mathews

BUSINESS STAFF

Vice President and Chief Operations Officer: Tom Siebenmorgen

Vice President, Sales and Marketing:
Pam Stebbins

Corporate Planning and Development Director: Laticia Dittrich

National Accounts Director:
Martha Adams

Sales and Services Director:
Margaret Reinold

Vice President, Operations:
Jim Dittrich

Comptroller, Operations:
Rob Thieme

Retail Customer Service Manager:
Stan Raynor

Print Production Manager:
Fred F. Pruss

ISBN-10: 1-60140-552-9
ISBN-13: 978-1-60140-552-4

table of contents

THE LEGEND OF THE DOGWOOD TREE

Folk tales and legends have sprung up through the centuries to illustrate God's ultimate sacrifice. This moving account of Jesus and the dogwood tree has found a fond place in the hearts of many.

Chart on page 28

FOOTPRINTS
This classic poem has given strength to weary souls for many decades. Let it hearten and reassure you that you are never alone.

Chart on page 32

TABLE GRACES

If you are fortunate enough to gather the family together at meal times, these cross stitch offerings of thanks and praise will keep everyone mindful of your most important dinner guest.

Charts on pages 82-88

THE LORD'S PRAYER
For nearly two millennia believers have followed this example of Christ's perfect prayer by offering praise, asking for necessities and protection, and acknowledging the power of God.

Chart on page 34

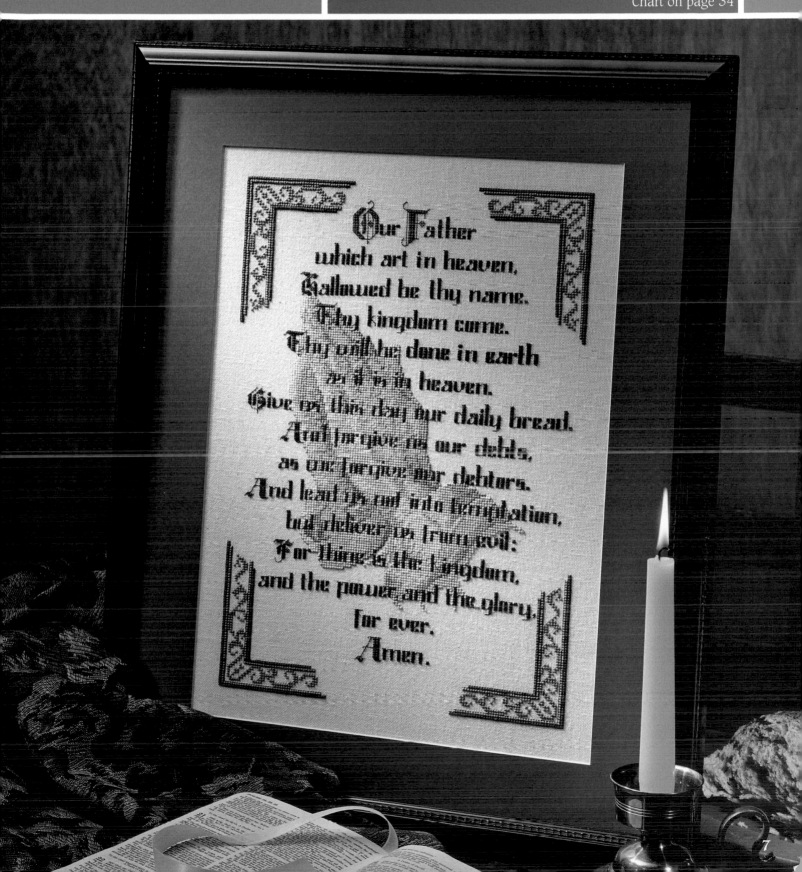

LOVE IS PATIENT

What better way to celebrate a marriage than to share these verses on the nature of love?

Chart on page 50

FOR WHITHER THOU GOEST
This verse from Ruth tells of a great love between two people and is perfect to share with a couple on their wedding day.

Chart on page 52

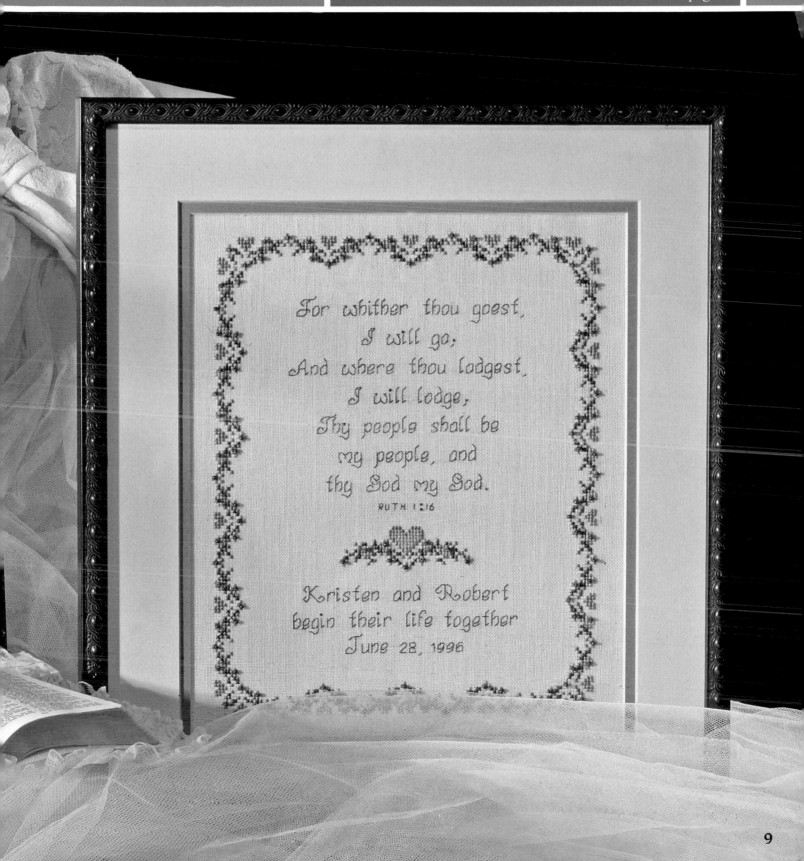

For whither thou goest,
I will go;
And where thou lodgest,
I will lodge,
Thy people shall be
my people, and
thy God my God.

RUTH 1:16

Kristen and Robert
begin their life together
June 28, 1996

THIS IS MY BELOVED
The gifts of friendship and love are always
worth celebrating!

Chart on page 56

LOVE ONE ANOTHER WITH A PURE HEART
Commemorate that special day with this reminder
of how we are to love one another.

Chart on page 54

SCRIPTURES FOR SPECIAL PEOPLE

Whether you are honoring a mother, daughter, or new parents, these scriptures will remind them of how special they are to God and to you.

Charts on pages 58-63

HEAVEN

They bring us laughter, celebrate our victories, and dry our tears. Our friends deserve no less than our support and devotion in their time of need. Bless the heart of a friend with this lovely sampler.

Chart on page 64

BEHOLD

To have a special friend is certainly a gift from God. Why not show how much their friendship means to you by stitching this piece that says it all.

Chart on page 66

God never loved me in such a way
til He brought thee
to me and said

Behold a Friend

THE LORD BLESS THEE

Remember a special person in your life with this beautiful sampler of Numbers 6:24.

Chart on page 38

THE PRAYER OF JABEZ
The prayer of Jabez is celebrated as an example of God's readiness to bring blessings to those who earnestly ask for them.

Chart on page 74

BOOKMARKS FROM THE PSALMS

Thoughtful gifts that will bring joy to the recipient, these bookmarks are stitched with some of the best-loved verses of the Bible.

Charts on pages 79-81

SPEAKING OF ANGELS

Stitching this special selection of verses from the Bible will remind us of the extraordinary nature of angels.

Chart on page 90

GLORIOUS EARTH

We have only to look at God's creation to know
how mighty is this King of kings.

Charts on pages 42-45

EVERY VALLEY

The glory of the Lord is truly revealed in this beautiful verse from Isaiah.

Chart on page 46

Every Valley shall be exalted, and Every Mountain & Hill shall be made low: and the Crooked shall be made Straight, and the Rough Places Plain: and the Glory of the Lord shall be Revealed

Isaiah 40:4-5

THE FATHER'S WONDROUS LOVE

In this busy world, we all need these reassurances that Love is not a concept, but the Lord God Himself.

Charts on pages 68-71

Behold what manner of love the Father hath bestowed upon us.
1 JOHN 3:1

Love

Ye shall abide in my love.
JOHN 15:10

24

BUT THEY THAT WAIT
Isaiah's perfect words for the weary believer,
illustrated with the eagle's strength and majesty.

Chart on page 72

PATRIOTIC HOLIDAYS
Our nation is a gift from the Lord. And when it sees troubling times, we must remember that God protects His children.

Chart on page 89

WE WENT THROUGH FIRE AND THROUGH WATER, YET THOU DIDST BRING US OUT INTO A PLACE OF ABUNDANCE. PS. 66:12

THE LEGEND OF THE DOGWOOD TREE

Stitch Count: 200 wide x 169 high

Project Information: The design was stitched on a 20½" x 18½" piece of 28 count Platinum Cashel Linen® over two fabric threads. It was custom framed.

Cross Stitch- 3 strands

Symbol	Color	DMC	Anchor
	white	blanc	2
	ecru	ecru	387
	vy dk green	319	218
	green	320	215
	dk salmon	347	1025
	dk green	367	217
	lt green	368	214
	vy lt green	369	1043
	grey	452	232
	dk yellow green	469	267
	yellow green	470	267
	lt yellow green	471	266
	vy lt yellow green	472	253
	dk taupe	640	903
	taupe	642	392
	lt taupe	644	830
	yellow	725	305
	lt yellow	726	295
	lt salmon	760	1022
	vy lt salmon	761	1021
	mint green	772	259
	cream	822	390
	dk brown	839	1086
	brown	840	1084
	lt brown	841	1082
	vy lt brown	842	1080
	forest green	890	218
	olive	935	861
	vy dk yellow green	937	268
	salmon	3712	1023

Blended Cross Stitch 2 strands of first color, 1 strand of second

Symbol	Color	DMC	Anchor
	lt grey & white	453 & blanc	231 & 2
	yellow & yellow green	725 & 470	305 & 267

Shaded areas indicate last rows stitched on opposite sections.

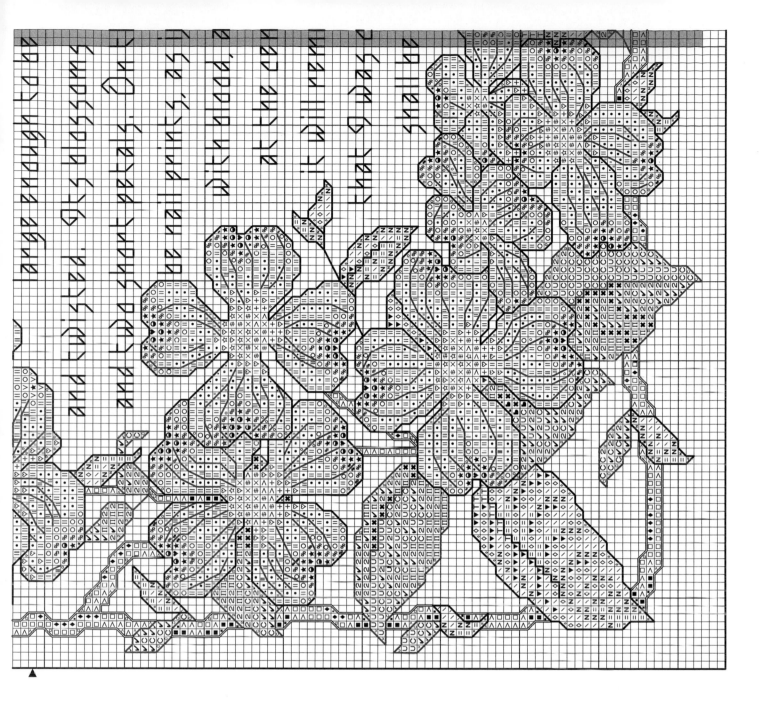

Backstitch – 1 strand

Symbol	Color
◿	dk brown
◿	dk salmon for title
◿	taupe for flowers
◿	olive for leaves
◿	dk taupe for flowers
◿	forest green for title, leaves, and leaf stems
◿	brown for wording

Design by Donna Vermillion Giampa.

Photo on page 4

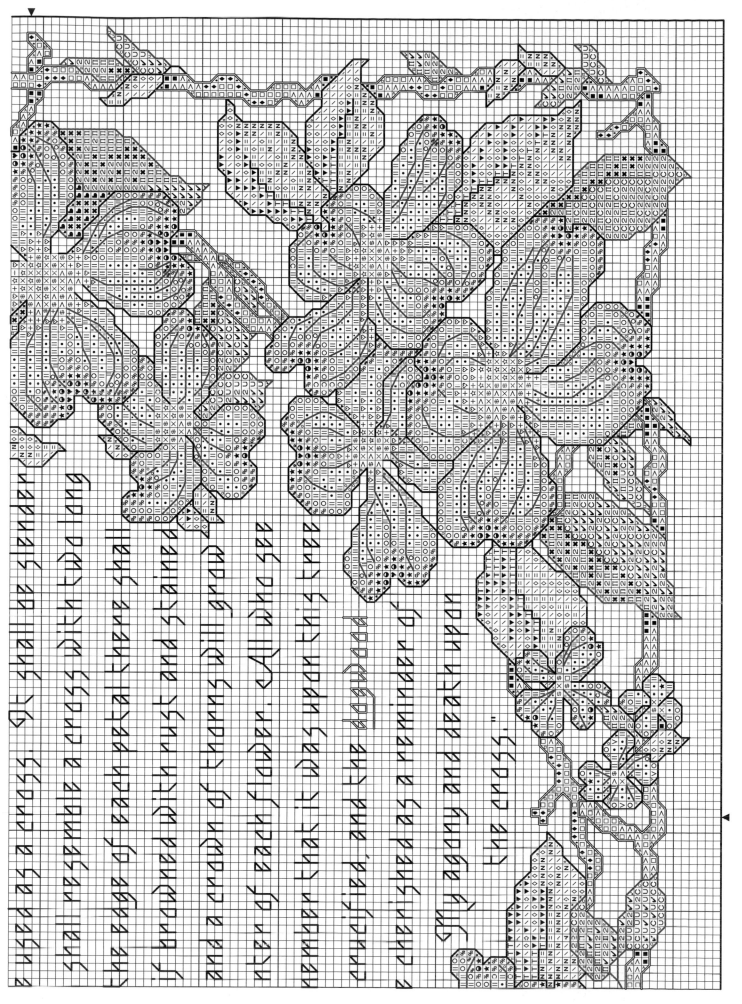

FOOTPRINTS

Stitch Count: 106 wide x 199 high

Project Information: The design was stitched on a 13" x 19" piece of 32 count Summer Khaki Belfast Linen over two fabric threads. It was custom framed.

Cross Stitch – 2 strands

Symbol	Color	DMC	Anchor
⊟	white	blanc	2
C	dk shell pink	221	897
◪	grey	318	399
V	dk grey	413	236
◣	lt grey	415	398
⊠	green	522	860
X	lt green	524	858
▢	lt salmon	760	1022
◐	vy lt grey	762	234
✦	vy dk brown grey	3021	905
■	brown grey	3022	8581
·	lt brown grey	3023	1040
●	dk green	3051	681
✖	steel grey	3072	847
⊘	dk salmon	3328	1024
❖	salmon	3712	1023
╱	shell pink	3721	896
＋	dk brown grey	3787	273

Half Cross Stitch – 1 strand

Symbol	Color	DMC	Anchor
◹	dk taupe	610	889
◲	taupe	611	898
Σ	lt taupe	612	832
✳	blue grey	927	848

Backstitch – 1 strand

Symbol	Color
╱	dk grey for seagulls
╱	vy dk brown grey for remaining backstitch

Design by Carol Emmer.

Shaded area indicates last row stitched on top section.

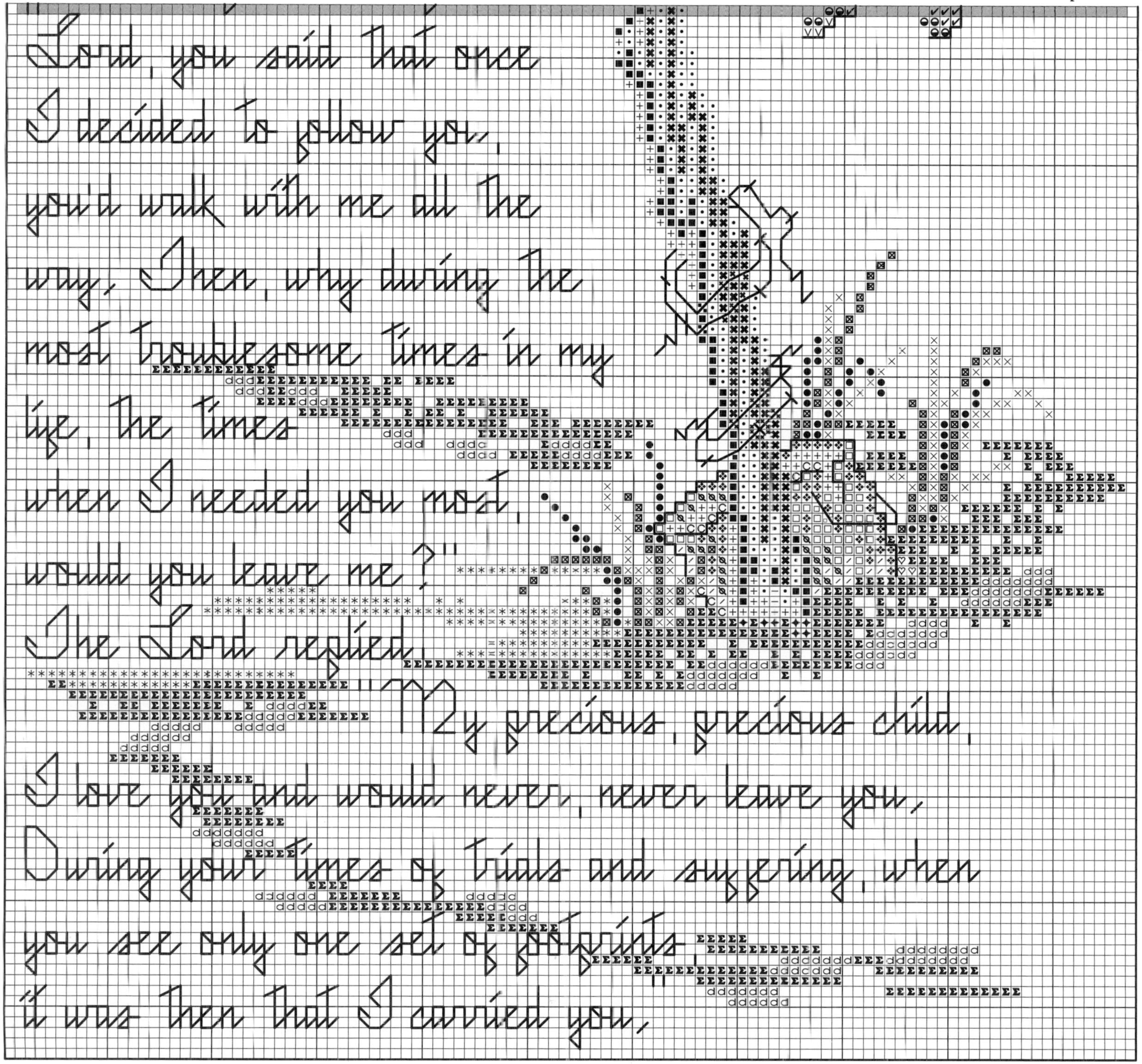

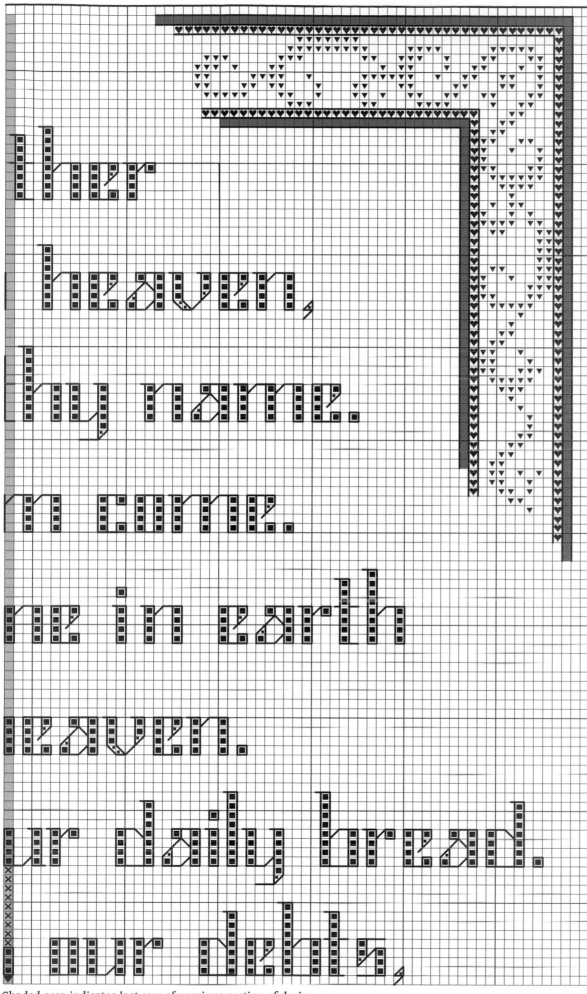

THE LORD'S PRAYER

Stitch Count:
140 wide x 206 high
Project Information:
The design was stitched on a 16" x 21" piece of 28 count Antique White Cashel Linen over two fabric threads. It was custom framed.

Cross Stitch – 3 strands

Symbol	Color	DMC
5	vy lt flesh	948
·	lt flesh	950
■	brown black	3371
♥	dk flesh	3772
✕	flesh	3773
▮	blue	3808
▼	lt blue	3810

Backstitch – 1 strand

Symbol	Color
⁄	brown black for wording and borders
⁄	dk flesh for hands

French Knot – 1 strand

Symbol	Color
●	brown black

Design by Terri Lee Steinmeyer.

Photo on page 7

Shaded area indicates last row of previous section of design.

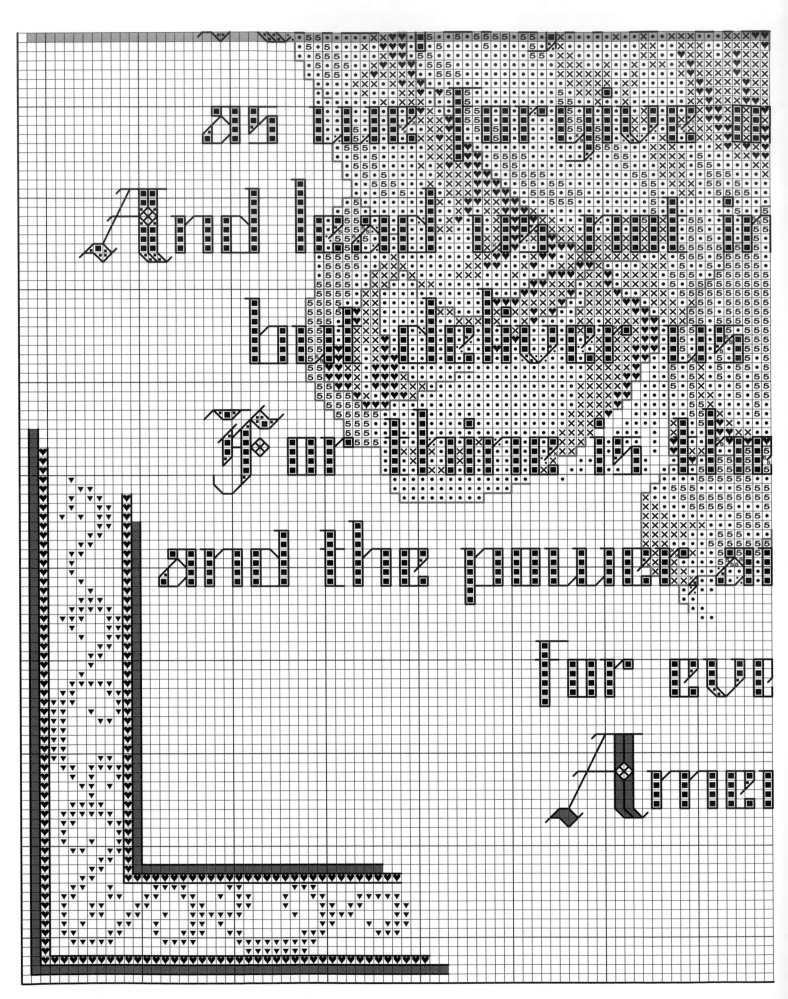

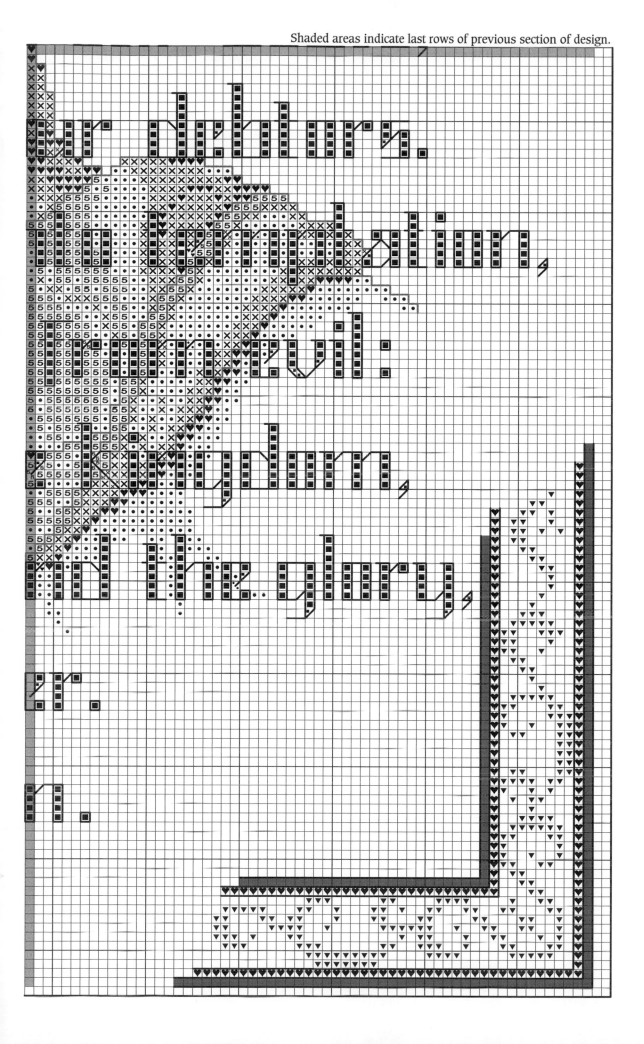

THE LORD BLESS THEE

Stitch Count: 89 wide x 137 high

Project Information:
The design was stitched on a 12½" x 16" piece of 28 count Natural Irish Linen over two fabric threads. It was custom framed.

Note: The chart is broken into 3 sections for ease in determining Backstitch colors. Backstitch notes list numbers of strands to use in parentheses. For example, "(2x)" means "use 2 strands."

Cross Stitch - All sections
Use 3 strands.

Symbol	Color	DMC	Anchor
◆	dk rose	221	897
2	lt rose	224	893
+	olive	580	281
✕	lt gold	676	891
◀	gold	729	890
⊙	dk gold	780	309
▶	beige	822	390
∧	blue	924	851
−	lt blue	926	850
□	lt green	3013	842
■	brown	3021	905
	green	3362	263
◑	rose	3722	1027
	lt brown	3790	393

Backstitch- Section 1
Symbol	Color
╱	lt brown (2x)
╱	dk rose (2x) for zigzag
╱	olive (2x) for top horizontal line and tulip vines
╱	gold (2x) for tulip pistils
╱	beige (2x) for tulips
╱	green (1x) for remaining Backstitch

Shaded area indicates first row stitched on bottom section.

38

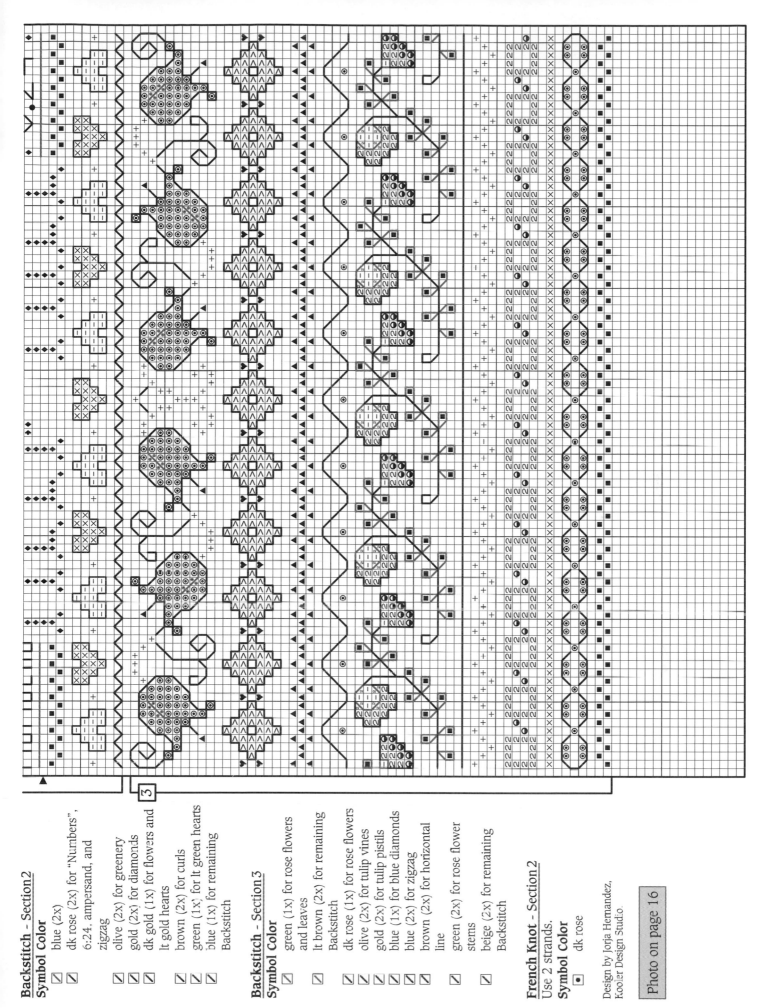

Backstitch – Section2
Symbol Color

Symbol	Color
∕	blue (2x)
∕	dk rose (2x) for "Numbers", 6:24. ampersand, and zigzag
∕	olive (2x) for greenery
∕	gold (2x) for diamonds
∕	dk gold (1x) for flowers and
∕	lt gold hearts
∕	brown (2x) for curls
∕	green (1x) for lt green hearts
∕	blue (1x) for remaining Backstitch

Backstitch – Section3
Symbol Color

Symbol	Color
∕	green (1x) for rose flowers and leaves
∕	lt brown (2x) for remaining Backstitch
∕	dk rose (1x) for rose flowers
∕	olive (2x) for tulip vines
∕	gold (2x) for tulip pistils
∕	blue (1x) for blue diamonds
∕	blue (2x) for zigzag
∕	brown (2x) for horizontal line
∕	green (2x) for rose flower stems
∕	beige (2x) for remaining Backstitch

French Knot – Section2
Use 2 strands.
Symbol Color

Symbol	Color
●	dk rose

Design by Jorja Hernandez,
Kooler Design Studio.

Photo on page 16

39

CHRISTMAS

Stitch Count:
93 wide x 162 high

Project Information: The design was stitched on a 13" x 18" piece of 14 count Antique White Aida. It was custom framed.

Cross Stitch – 3 strands

Symbol	Color	DMC	Anchor
✖	rose brown	632	936
◉	lt gold	676	891
★	flesh	758	868
▶	gold	783	306
◤	sky blue	800	144
◯	dk blue	930	1035
·	blue	931	1034
	lt blue	932	1033
◺	lt flesh	945	881
■	brown	975	355
◻	baby blue	3756	1037
⬒	lt rose brown	3772	1007
	dk flesh	3778	1013
	vy lt gold	3823	386

Three-Quarter Stitch – 3 strands

Symbol	Color	DMC	Anchor
◢	lt rose brown	3772	1007
	dk flesh	3778	1013

Backstitch – 1 strand

Symbol	Color
	lt rose brown
	dk blue
	rose brown for Infant's face
	blue for clothing
	gold for star & rays (long stitches)
	brown for remaining backstitch

Design by Linda Gillum, Kooler Design Studio.

Photo on page 21

Shaded area indicates last row stitched on top section.

THE GRASS WITHERETH

Stitch Count: 98 wide x 67 high

Project Information: The design was stitched on a 13" x 11" piece of 28 count Smokey Pearl Cashel Linen® over two fabric threads. It was custom framed.

Cross Stitch – 3 strands

Symbol	Color	DMC	Anchor
⊡	white	blanc	2
✳	dk khaki	370	855
♡	khaki	371	854
◉	lt khaki	372	853
⊠	brown	433	358
▽	lt brown	435	1046
8	dk blue green	500	683
H	blue green	501	878
▼	lt blue green	502	877
✔	vy lt blue green	503	876
C	grey	644	830
◎	yellow	725	305
%	lt yellow green	772	259
4	dk gold	781	308
❖	gold	783	306
Π	hazel brown	829	906
	dk blue	924	851
▷	lt blue	926	850
‖	vy lt blue	927	848
Σ	vy dk green	934	862
⊠	dk brown	938	381
	grey green	3013	842
◇	violet	3041	871
$	lt violet	3042	870
★	yellow green	3348	264
∅	dk green	3362	263
2	green	3363	262
⬠	lt green	3364	260
■	dk violet	3740	873
T	vy lt violet	3743	869
5	blue	3768	779
◈	lt gold	3820	306
◣	vy lt gold	3822	295

Half Cross Stitch – 1 strand

Symbol	Color	DMC	Anchor
=	dk blue	924	851
╲	lt blue	926	850
▢	vy lt blue	927	848
+	blue	3768	779

Backstitch – 1 strand

Symbol	Color
╱	grey for grass (long stitches)
╱	dk blue green for Scripture and Reference
╱	grey green for grass (long stitches)

French Knot – 1 strand

Symbol	Color
•	dk blue green

Design by Donna Vermillion Giampa.

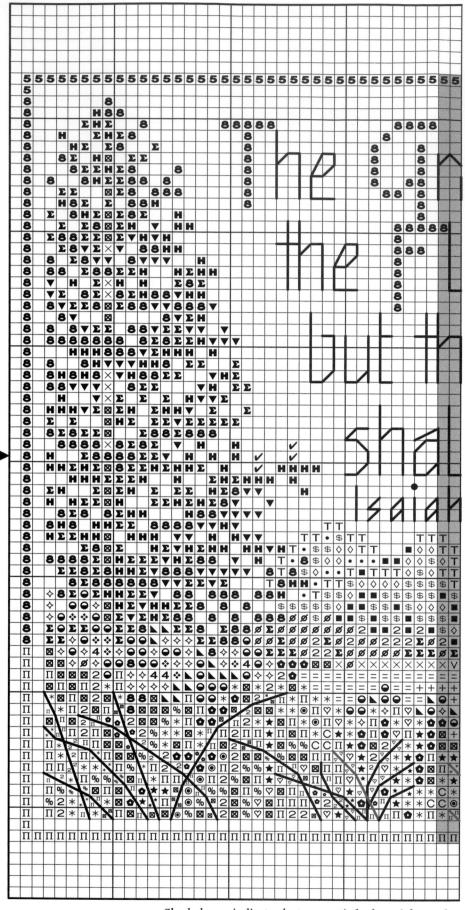

Shaded area indicates last rows stitched on right section.

Photo on page 22

AND THINE EARS SHALL HEAR

Stitch Count: 110 wide x 78 high

Project Information: The design was stitched on a 14" x 12" piece of 28 count Confederate Grey Cashel Linen® over two fabric threads. It was custom framed.

Cross Stitch – 3 strands

Symbol	Color	DMC	Anc.
⊙	white	blanc	2
◖	grey	413	236
<	dk green	469	267
‖	green	470	267
✳	lt green	471	266
–	vy lt green	472	253
◉	blue green	500	683
	grey green	522	860
	lt grey green	524	858
◊	topaz	725	305
⊕	lt topaz	727	293
8	dk topaz	783	306
✦	brown	801	359
◣	gold	832	907
╱	dk brown	898	360
⊠	orange	922	1003
§	grey blue	926	850
5	lt grey blue	927	848
Σ	forest green	935	861
U	vy dk green	937	268
%	peach	945	881
♥	dk rust	975	355
▲	dk khaki green	3011	846
♡	khaki green	3012	844
2	lt khaki green	3013	842
◪	mocha brown	3021	905
L	brown grey	3022	8581
★	lt brown grey	3023	1040
△	vy lt brown grey	3024	397
▪	brown black	3371	382
	dk brown grey	3787	273
¢	yellow	3822	295
✕	rust	3826	1049
>	lt rust	3827	311

Half Cross Stitch – 1 strand

Symbol	Color	DMC	Anc.
•	dk green	469	267
O	green	470	267
✧	lt green	471	266
\	blue green	500	683
+	grey green	522	860
4	lt grey green	524	858
T	brown	801	359
∏	gold	832	907
E	forest green	935	861
✔	dk khaki green	3011	846
d	khaki green	3012	844
V	lt khaki green	3013	842

Backstitch – 1 strand

Symbol	Color
╱	dk brown for branches
╱	dk brown grey for tree and Scripture
╱	mocha brown for Scripture
╱	brown grey for remaining backstitch
╱	grey for tree trunks
╱	brown black for remaining backstitch

French Knot – 1 strand

Symbol	Color
⊙	dk brown grey
⊙	mocha brown
⊙	brown black

Design by Donna Vermillion Giampa.

Photo on page 22

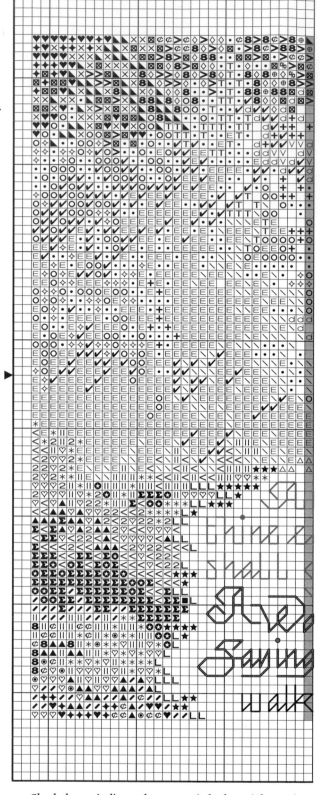

Shaded area indicates last row stitched on right section.

EVERY VALLEY

Stitch Count: 158 wide x 142 high

Project Information: The design was stitched on a 17¹⁄₂" x 16¹⁄₂" piece of 28 count Confederate Grey Cashel Linen® over two fabric threads. It was custom framed.

Photo on page 23

Design by Donna Vermillion Giampa.

Cross Stitch – 3 strands

Symbol	Color	DMC	Anchor
⊡	white	blanc	2
■	black	310	403
◉	dk blue	312	979
T	blue	322	978
◖	vy dk blue	336	150
◢	vy dk blue green	500	683
◆	dk blue green	501	878
⊕	blue green	502	877

Cross Stitch – 3 strands

Symbol	Color	DMC	Anchor
$	lt blue green	503	876
◆	vy lt blue green	504	1042
∅	dk green	520	862
4	green	522	860
%	lt green	523	859
–	vy lt green	524	858
☆	dk grey	645	273
●	grey	646	8581

Cross Stitch – 3 strands

Symbol	Color	DMC	Anchor
▽	lt grey	647	1040
L	vy lt grey	648	900
‖‖	beige	822	390
♥	vy dk grey	844	1041
□	vy dk blue grey	924	851
✦	blue grey	926	850
○	lt blue grey	927	848
△	vy lt blue grey	928	274

Cross Stitch – 3 strands

Symbol	Color	DMC	Anchor
✔	vy dk green	934	862
⊙	vy dk brown	3031	905
✕	brown	3032	903
◁	vy lt brown	3033	391
▷	pearl grey	3072	847
=	vy lt blue	3325	129
⊠	grey green	3363	262
C	lt blue	3755	140

Cross Stitch – 3 strands

Symbol	Color	DMC	Anchor
♡	dk blue grey	3768	779
✚	dk brown	3781	904
✳	lt brown	3782	899
✦	mint green	3813	875

Backstitch – 1 strand

Symbol	Color
╱	black for facial features

Backstitch – 1 strand

Symbol	Color
╱	dk blue green for Scripture
╱	blue green for Scripture and Reference
╱	vy dk blue green for Scripture
╱	vy dk brown for wolves

French Knot – 1 strand

Symbol	Color
⊙	white

Shaded area indicates last row stitched on opposite section.

Shaded areas indicate last rows stitched on opposite sections.

LOVE IS PATIENT

Stitch Count: 123 wide x 159 high

Project Information: The design was stitched on a 15" x 17½" piece of 28 count Cream Cashel Linen® over two fabric threads. It was custom framed. To personalize design, use dk green and refer to alphabet 3 and numbers, page 54.

Cross Stitch – 3 strands

Symbol	Color	DMC	Anchor
✧	blue grey	926	850
■	lt mauve	3354	74
·	dk green	3362	263
	green	3363	262
✖	mauve	3688	66
▨	dk mauve	3803	972

Backstitch – 1 strand

Symbol	Color
∕	blue grey for stems
∕	dk green for Scripture and Reference
∕	dk mauve for remaining backstitch

French Knot – 1 strand

Symbol	Color
•	dk green

Beads

Symbol	Color
◎	Mill Hill Glass Seed Bead #02012 royal plum

Design by Mary Scott.

Photo on page 8

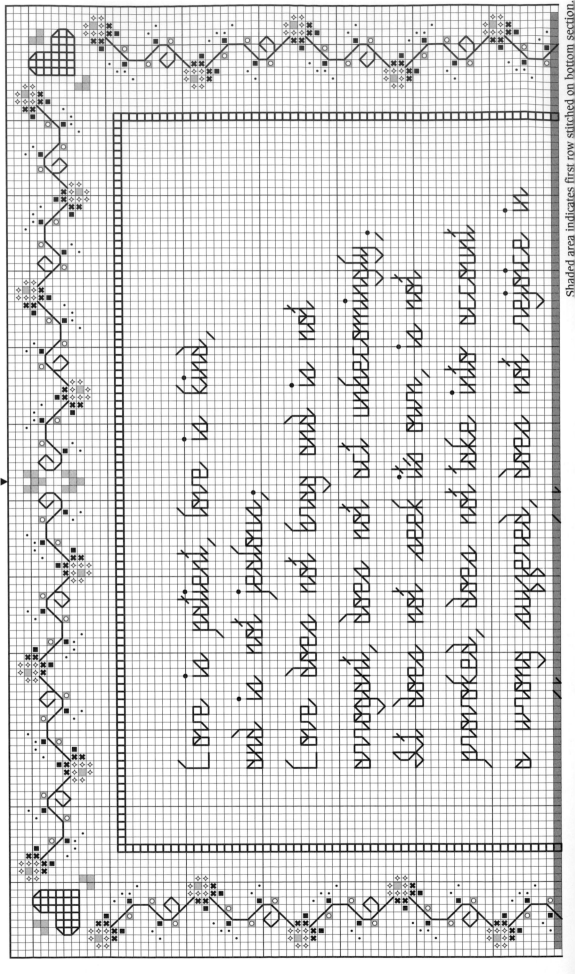

Shaded area indicates first row stitched on bottom section.

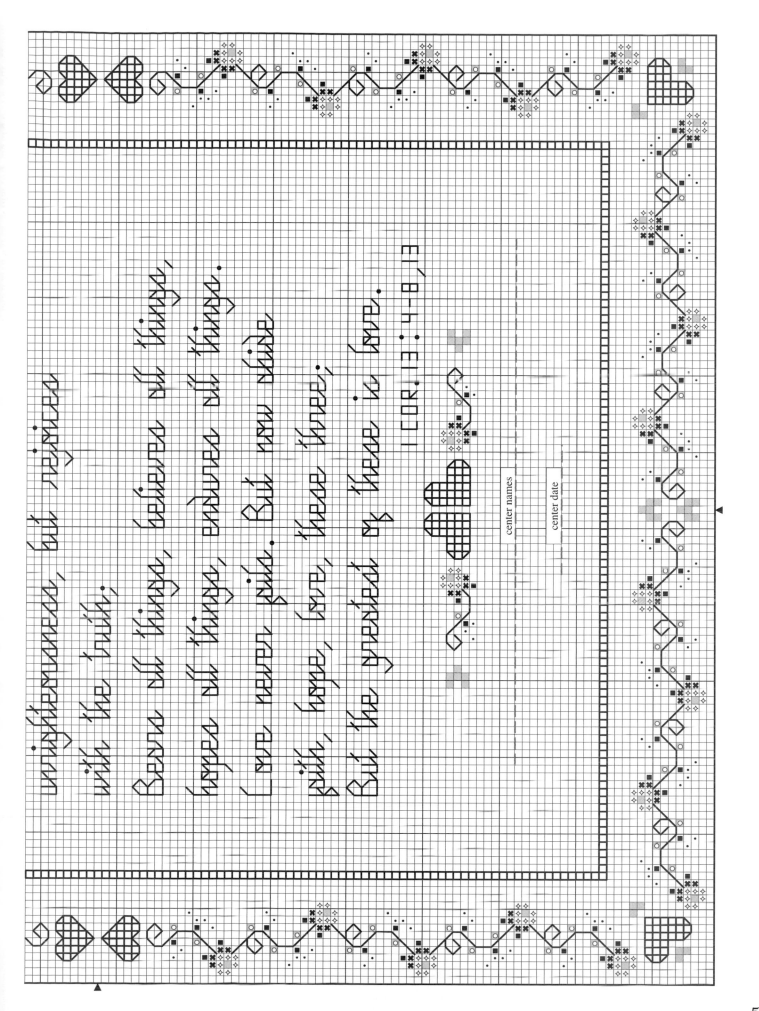

center names

center date

FOR WHITHER THOU GOEST

Stitch Count: 123 wide x 149 high

Project Information: The design was stitched on a 15" x 16³/₄" piece of 28 count Cream Cashel Linen® over two fabric threads. It was custom framed. To personalize design, use green and refer to alphabets 1, 2, and numbers, page 54.

Cross Stitch – 3 strands

Symbol	Color	DMC	Anchor
☒	lt green	522	860
⊪	lt mauve	3354	74
◩	green	3362	263
▨	dk mauve	3687	68
◁	mauve	3688	66

Backstitch – 1 strand

Symbol	Color
◿	green

French Knot – 1 strand

Symbol	Color
•	green

Beads

Symbol	Color
⊙	Mill Hill Glass Seed Bead #02012 royal plum

Design by Mary Scott.

Photo on page 9

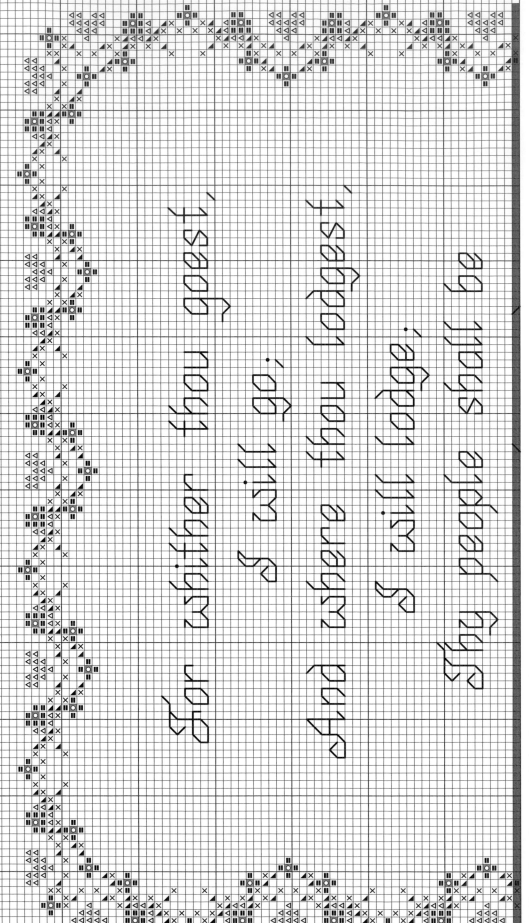

Shaded line indicates first row stitched on bottom section.

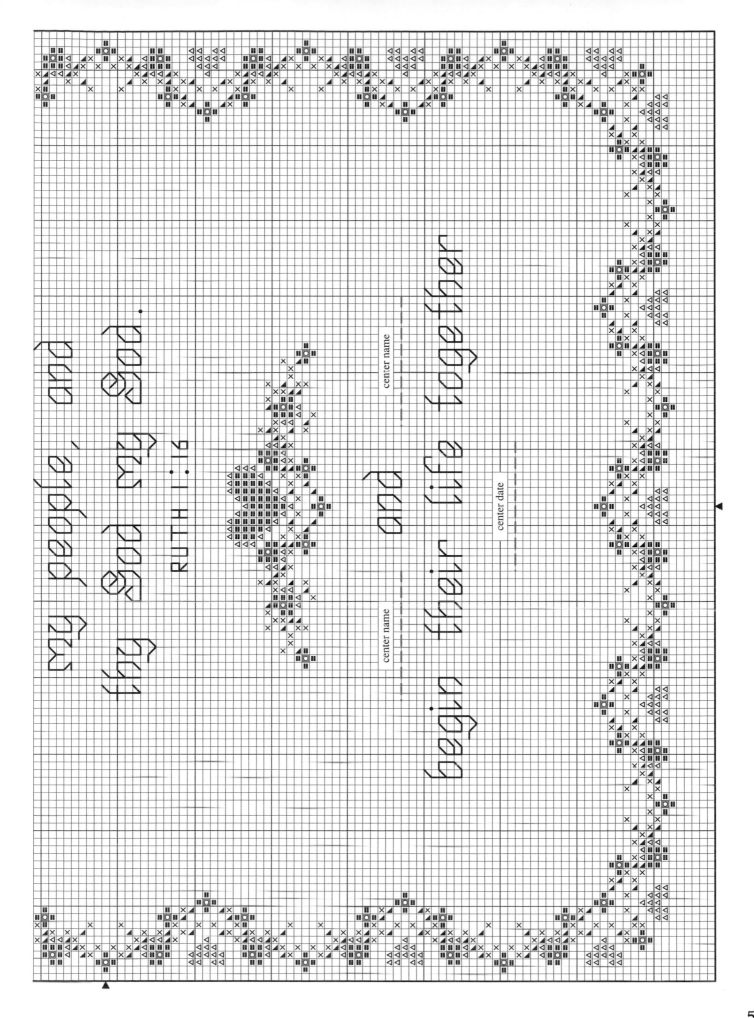

thy people and

thy God my God.

RUTH 1:16

center name

and

center name

center date

begin their life together

LOVE ONE ANOTHER WITH A PURE HEART

Stitch Count:
87 wide x 111 high

Project Information:
The design was stitched on a 12¼" x 14" piece of 28 count Cream Cashel Linen® over two fabric threads. It was custom framed. To personalize design, use two strands of dk blue grey and refer to alphabets 1, 2, and numbers on this page.

Cross Stitch – 3 strands

Symbol	Color	DMC	Anchor
·	white	blanc	2
▢	mauve	316	1017
◼	lt green	524	858
◉	lt mauve	778	968
✳	dk blue grey	926	850
▯	blue grey	927	848
❖	green	3363	262
▥	dk mauve	3726	1018

Photo on page 11

Backstitch

Symbol	Color
✒	mauve for flowers - 1 strand
✒	dk blue grey for Scripture and Reference - 1 strand
✒	lt green for stems - 2 strands
✒	blue grey for running stitch - 2 strands

French Knot – 1 strand

Symbol	Color
●	dk blue grey

Beads

Symbol	Color
◎	Mill Hill Glass Seed Bead #00553 old rose

Design by Mary Scott.

1
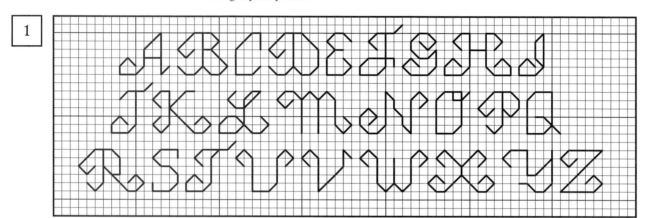

2
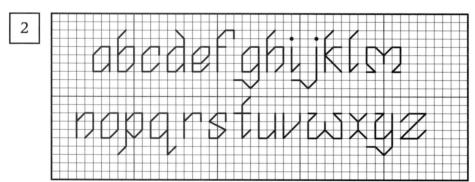

3
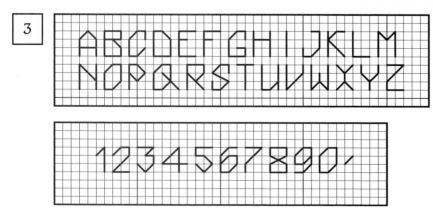

I PETER 1:22

center name   center name

center date

THIS IS MY BELOVED

Stitch Count: 95 wide x 123 high

Project Information: The design was stitched on a 13" x 15" piece of 28 count Cream Cashel Linen® over two fabric threads. It was custom framed. To personalize design, use one strand of blue grey and refer to alphabet 3 and numbers, page 54.

Photo on page 10

Cross Stitch – 3 strands

Symbol	Color	DMC	Anchor
■	mauve	316	1017
·	lt green	524	858
∥	lt mauve	778	968
◇	blue grey	926	850
✛	green	3363	262

Cross Stitch – 3 strands

Symbol	Color	DMC	Anchor
■	dk mauve	3726	1018

Backstitch

Symbol	Color
╱	blue grey - 2 strands

Backstitch

Symbol	Color
╱	blue grey - 1 strand

French Knot – 1 strand

Symbol	Color
·	blue grey

Design by Mary Scott.

Shaded area indicates first row stitched on bottom section.

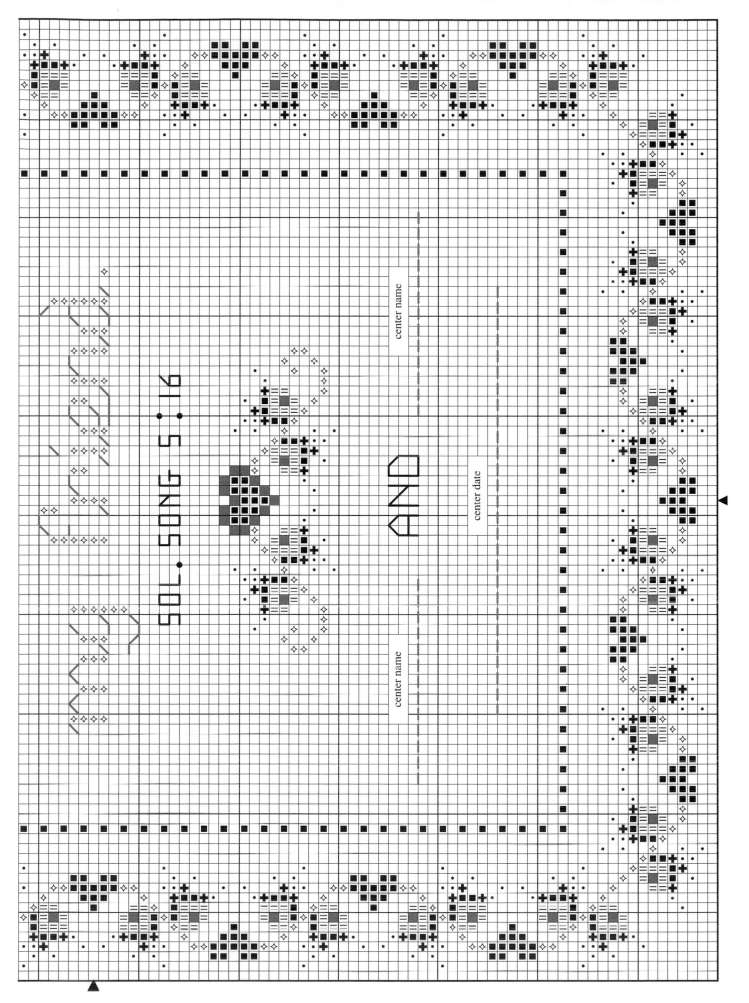

center name

center date

AND

center name

SONG 5:16

NEW PARENTS

Stitch Count: 103 wide x 103 high

Project Information: The design was stitched on a 13¹/₂" x 13¹/₂" piece of 14 count White Aida. It was custom framed.

Cross Stitch – 2 strands

Symbol	Color	DMC	Anchor
•	white	blanc	2
Π	lavender	209	109
⊙	dk lavender	552	99
P	dk aqua	597	1064
☆	aqua	598	1062
□	fuchsia	604	55
▼	lt fuchsia	605	1094
5	plum	718	88
	orange	741	304
◣	flesh	754	1012
*	pink	761	1021
■	dk rust	780	309
=	lt flesh	948	1011
8	rust	976	1001
>	lt pink	3713	1020
◖	baby blue	3756	1037
✕	dk fuchsia	3806	62
Σ	lt aqua	3811	1060
−	lt rust	3827	311

Blended Cross Stitch – 2 strands of floss, 1 strand of Kreinik Blending Filament

Symbol	Color	DMC & Kreinik		Anchor & Kreinik	
‖	white & pearl	blanc	& 032	2	& 032
T	lavender & lilac	209	& 023	109	& 023
✕	lt lavender & pearl	211	& 032	342	& 032
♥	lt fuchsia & pearl	605	& 032	1094	& 032
V	yellow & gold	744	& 002HL	301	& 002HL

Backstitch – 1 strand

Symbol	Color
╱	dk rust
╱	lavender for wings and collar
╱	dk lavender for "of the Lord" and "Ps. 127:3"
╱	dk aqua for baby blanket
╱	plum for "are a heritage"
╱	orange for halo
╱	dk fuchsia for "Lo, children," dress, and lips

French Knot – 1 strand

Symbol	Color
⊙	dk lavender

Design by Barbara Baatz Hillman, Kooler Design Studio.

Photo on page 13

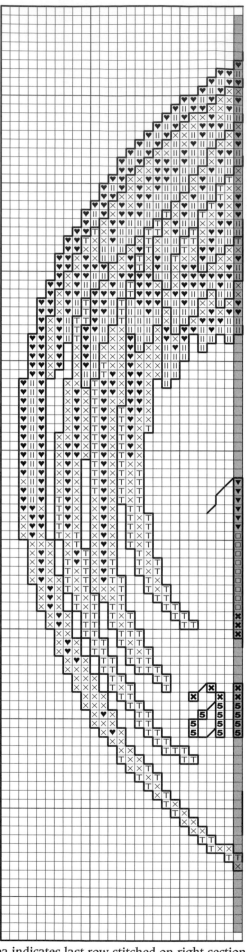

Shaded area indicates last row stitched on right section.

MOTHER

Stitch Count: 104 wide x 104 high

Project Information: The design was stitched on a 13¹/₂" x 13¹/₂" piece of 28 count Tea-Dyed Irish Linen over two fabric threads. It was custom framed.

Cross Stitch – 3 strands

Symbol	Color	DMC	Anchor
⊡	white	blanc	2
	green	367	217
✳	lt green	368	214
⊘	aqua	597	1064
♥	gold	676	891
⊙	lt blue	813	161
✦	blue	826	161
$	grey blue	932	1033
⊠	pink	956	40
+	lt pink	957	50
○	lt rust	977	1002
⧹	lavender	3042	870
□	lt grey blue	3752	1032
■	charcoal grey	3799	236
✖	dk aqua	3809	1066
⬟	mint green	3817	875
%	yellow	3823	386
⧹	rust	3826	1049

Backstitch – 1 strand

Symbol	Color
∕	green
∕	pink for buds
∕	charcoal grey for bills on baby swans, mask on large swan, eyes, and wording
∕	rust for swans and bill on large swan

French Knot – 1 strand

Symbol	Color
●	white for eyes
●	charcoal grey for wording

Design by Linda Gillum, Kooler Design Studio.

Photo on page 12

Shaded area indicates last row stitched on right section.

DAUGHTER

Stitch Count:
95 wide x 118 high

Project Information:
The design was stitched on a 13" x 14½" piece of 14 count Antique White Aida. It was custom framed.

Cross Stitch – 3 strands

Symbol	Color	DMC	Anchor
·	white	blanc	2
★	lavender	208	110
I	lt lavender	209	109
↙	lt red	304	1006
⊙	black	310	403
✚	dk pink	335	38
⁄	brown	434	310
	dk brown	436	1045
■	dk lavender	550	102
▶	dk green	561	212
	orange	741	304

Cross Stitch – 3 strands

Symbol	Color	DMC	Anchor
▣	dk brown	801	359
✿	dk red	814	45
↺	red	815	43
✕	blue	932	1033
∰	lt pink	963	73
❖	pink	3326	36
⊞	yellow green	3347	266
★	lt yellow green	3348	264
▷	lt blue	3753	1031
⊘	lt green	3813	875
	green	3816	876

Backstitch – 1 strand

Symbol	Color
☑	black for pansy centers (long stitches)
☑	dk lavender for pansy petals
☑	dk green for leaves and buds
☑	dk brown for heart
☑	lt red for "Pro. 31:29"
☑	dk red for wording
☑	red for rose and rosebuds
☑	blue for pansies
☑	brown for remaining backstitch

French Knot – 1 strand

Symbol	Color
⊙	lt red for "Pro. 31:29"
⊙	dk red for wording

Design by Barbara Baatz Hillman, Kooler Design Studio.

Photo on page 12

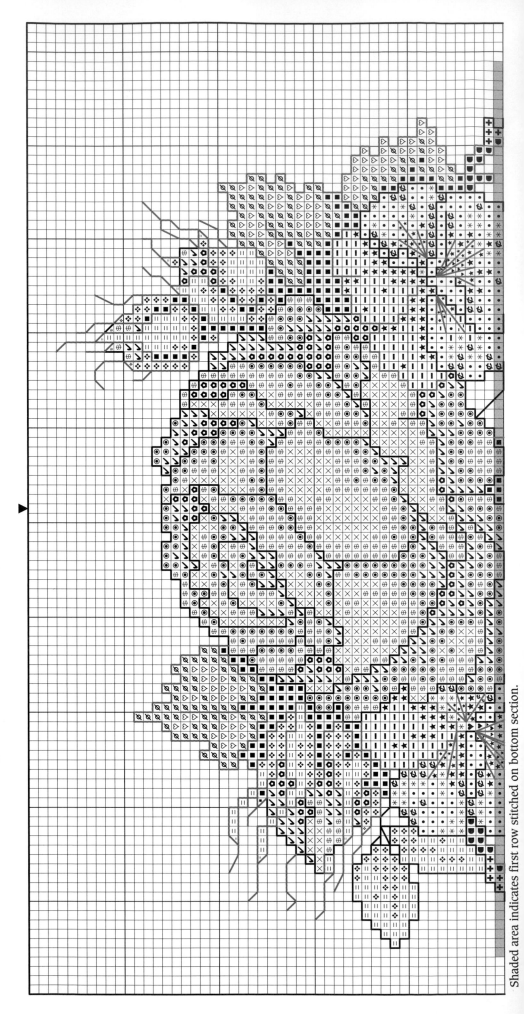

Shaded area indicates first row stitched on bottom section.

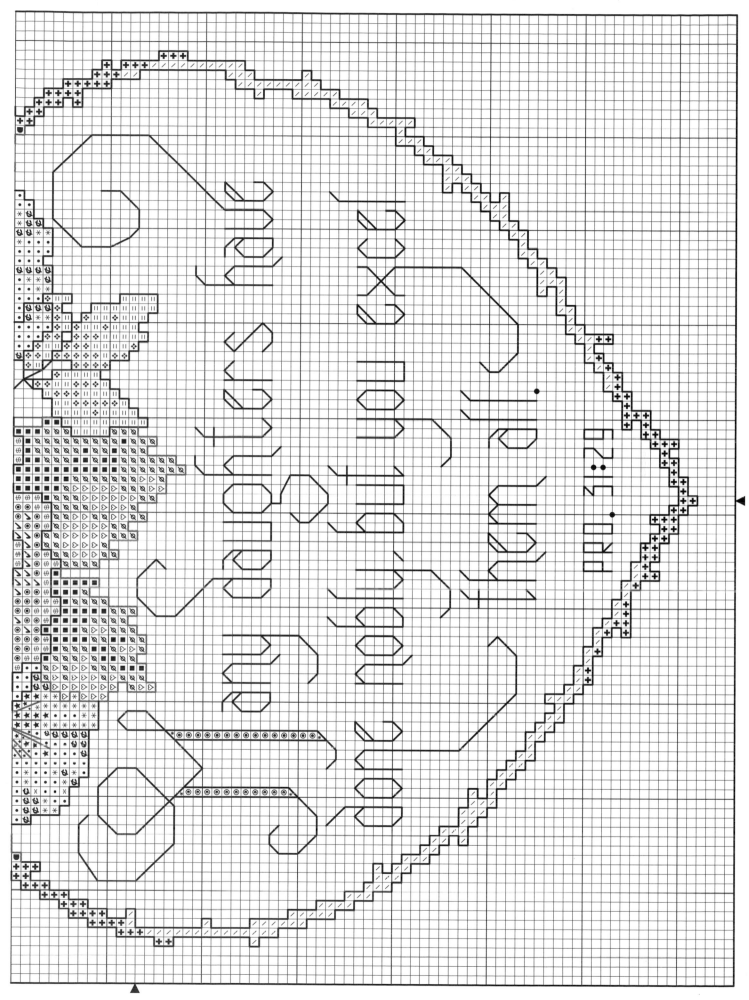

HEAVEN

Stitch Count: 140 wide x 112 high

Project Information: The design was stitched on a 16" x 14" piece of 28 count Cream Irish Linen over two fabric threads. It was custom framed.

Cross Stitch - 3 strands

Symbol	Color	DMC	Anchor
✿	grey	413	236
▽	lt salmon	761	1021
✖	blue	794	175
◉	lt pink	818	23
☆	dk green	937	268
■	green	3012	844
＝	lt green	3013	842
∏	salmon	3328	1024
✚	pink	3708	31

Backstitch - 1 strand

Symbol	Color
╱	lt salmon
╱	blue
╱	lt green
╱	green
╱	salmon

French Knot - 1 strand

Symbol	Color
●	salmon

Design by Jorja Hernandez, Kooler Design Studio.

Photo on page 14

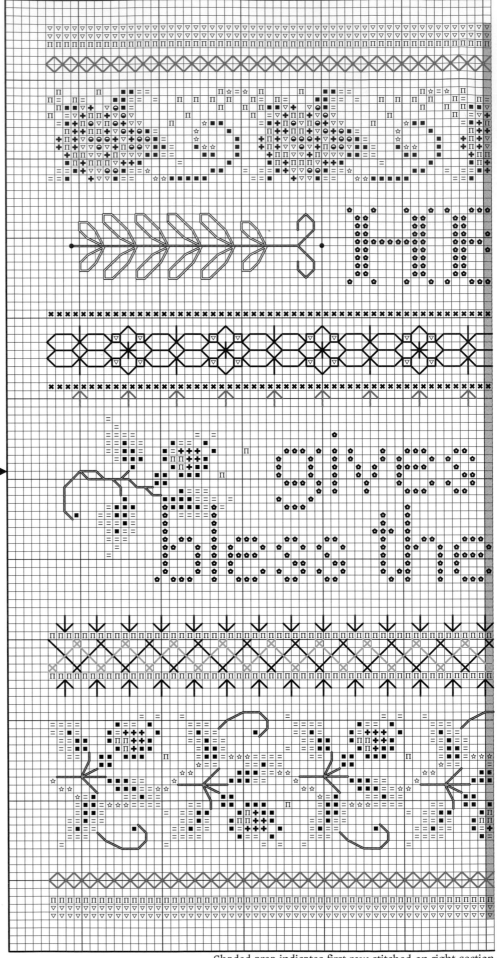

Shaded area indicates first row stitched on right section.

BEHOLD

Stitch Count: 136 wide x 93 high

Project Information: The design was stitched on a 16" x 13" piece of 28 count Tea-Dyed Irish Linen over two fabric threads. It was custom framed.

Cross Stitch - 3 strands

Symbol	Color	DMC	Anchor
•	white	blanc	2
Σ	dk peach	352	9
◤	peach	353	6
▪	grey	413	236
❖	salmon	760	1022
♡	lt salmon	761	1021
★	dk salmon	3328	1024
‖	green	3363	262
╱	lt green	3364	260
	dk grey	3799	236

Backstitch - 1 strand

Symbol	Color
╱	green
╱	salmon
╱	dk grey for "Behold A Friend"
╱	grey for remaining Backstitch

Backstitch - 2 strands

Symbol	Color
╱	green for wording

Design by Jorja Hernandez, Kooler Design Studio.

Photo on page 15

Shaded area indicates first row stitched on right section.

BEHOLD WHAT MANNER OF LOVE

Stitch Count: 89 wide x 117 high

Project Information: The design was stitched on a 13" x 15" piece of 28 count Antique White Cashel Linen over two fabric threads. It was custom framed.

Photo on page 24

Cross Stitch – 3 strands

Symbol	Color	DMC	Anchor
☑	green	502	877
✎	yellow	744	301
▶	blue	931	1034
■	mauve	3687	68

Design by Mary Scott.

Cross Stitch – 3 strands

Symbol	Color	DMC	Anchor
↗	lt mauve	3688	66
○	vy lt mauve	3689	49
☒	lt blue	3752	1032

Backstitch

Symbol	Color
╱	blue for "Love" - 2 strands
╱	blue for Reference - 1 strand

French Knot – 1 strand

Symbol	Color
⊙	blue

Shaded area indicates 1 row overlap.

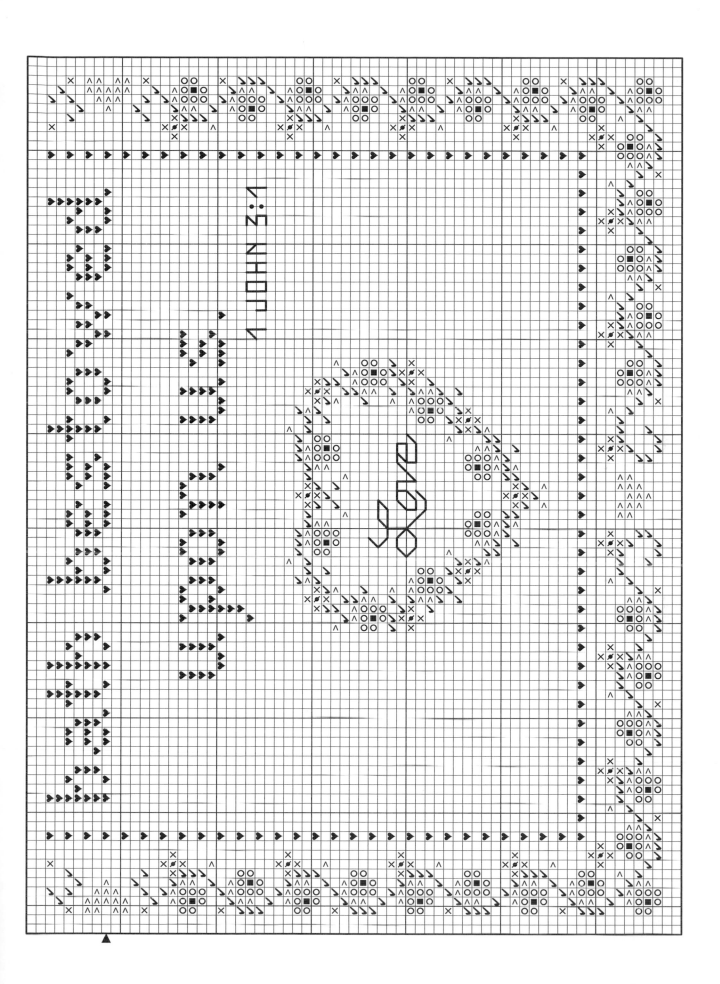

YE SHALL ABIDE IN MY LOVE

Stitch Count: 75 wide x 47 high

Project Information: The design was stitched on a 12" x 10" piece of 28 count Antique White Cashel Linen over two fabric threads. It was custom framed.

Cross Stitch – 3 strands

Symbol	Color	DMC	Anchor
▶	green	502	877
✕	lt green	503	876
○	mauve	3688	66
↘	dk mauve	3803	972

Design by Mary Scott.

Backstitch

Symbol	Color
↗	green for Scripture - 2 strands
↗	green for Reference - 1 strand
↗	dk mauve for border - 1 strand

French Knot – 1 strand

Symbol	Color
•	green

Photo on page 24

Ye shall abide in my love

JOHN 15:10

70

GOD IS LOVE

Stitch Count: 53 wide x 81 high

Project Information: The design was stitched on a 10" x 12" piece of 28 count Antique White Cashel Linen over two fabric threads. It was custom framed.

Photo on page 25

Cross Stitch – 3 strands

Symbol	Color	DMC	Anchor
⊠	green	502	877
♥	lt green	503	876
◣	mauve	3687	68
✔	lt mauve	3688	66
⊳	vy lt mauve	3689	49

Backstitch – 1 strand

Symbol	Color
✓	green

French Knot – 1 strand

Symbol	Color
•	green

Design by Mary Scott.

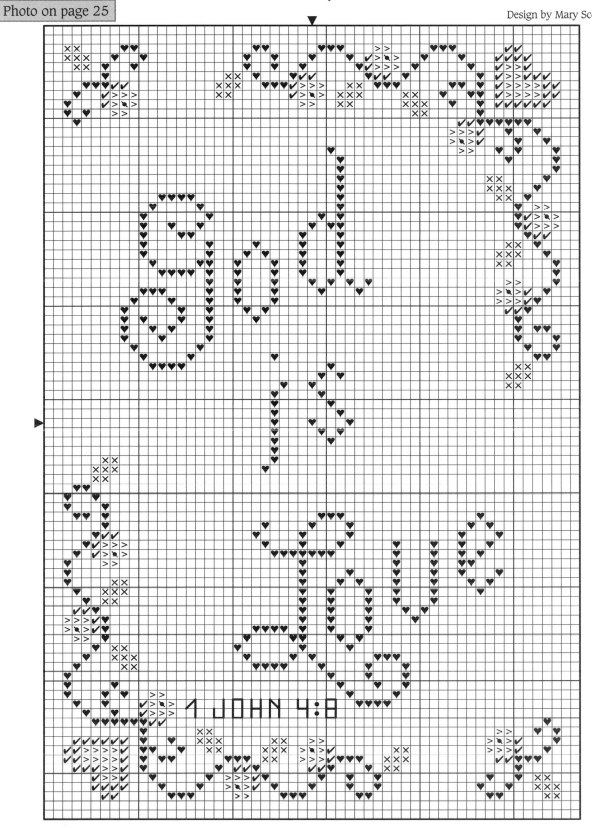

BUT THEY THAT WAIT

Stitch Count: 122 wide x 111 high

Project Information: The design was stitched on a 15" x 14" piece of 28 count Confederate Grey Cashel Linen® over two fabric threads. It was custom framed.

Cross Stitch – 3 strands

Symbol	Color	DMC	Anchor
⊙	white	blanc	2
H	black	310	403
▲	shell grey	451	233
⊳	lt shell grey	452	232
☆	vy dk blue green	500	683
◣	dk blue green	501	878
▽	blue green	502	877
2	lt blue green	503	876
◆	vy lt grey green	524	858
★	dk taupe	610	889
∅	taupe	611	898
♥	lt taupe	612	832
✖	vy lt taupe	613	831
	hazel brown	869	944
⊠	dk green	895	1044
	vy dk blue grey	924	851
	blue grey	926	850
	lt blue grey	927	848
	vy lt blue grey	928	274
Π	brown	938	381
T	vy dk brown grey	3021	905
◆	brown grey	3022	8581
✚	lt brown grey	3023	1040
◉	vy lt brown grey	3024	397
◈	yellow beige	3046	887
Σ	lt yellow beige	3047	852
	dk grey green	3051	681
	grey green	3052	262
	lt grey green	3053	261
✔	grey	3072	847
4	green	3362	263
▼	lt green	3363	262
%	vy lt green	3364	260
	brown black	3371	382
	violet	3743	869
	dk blue grey	3768	779
8	dk brown grey	3787	273
◖	lt hazel brown	3828	373

Cross Stitch – 1 strand

Symbol	Color	DMC	Anchor
▢	white	blanc	2
✿	shell grey	451	233
O	lt shell grey	452	232
$	vy dk blue grey	924	851
d	blue grey	926	850
5	lt blue grey	927	848
V	violet	3743	869
◉	dk blue grey	3768	779

Half Cross Stitch – 1 strand

Symbol	Color	DMC	Anchor
✕	vy dk blue grey	924	851
=	blue grey	926	850
◺	lt blue grey	927	848
+	vy lt blue grey	928	274
C	dk grey green	3051	681
*	grey green	3052	262
◇	lt grey green	3053	261
▽	dk blue grey	3768	779

Backstitch – 1 strand

Symbol	Color
╱	dk blue grey
╱	black for eye and talons
╱	dk taupe for Scripture and Reference
╱	hazel brown for beak and feet
╱	dk brown grey for head and white tail feathers
╱	brown black for remaining backstitch

French Knot – 1 strand

Symbol	Color
⊙	dk blue grey
◦	dk taupe

Design by Donna Vermillion Giampa.

Photo on page 26

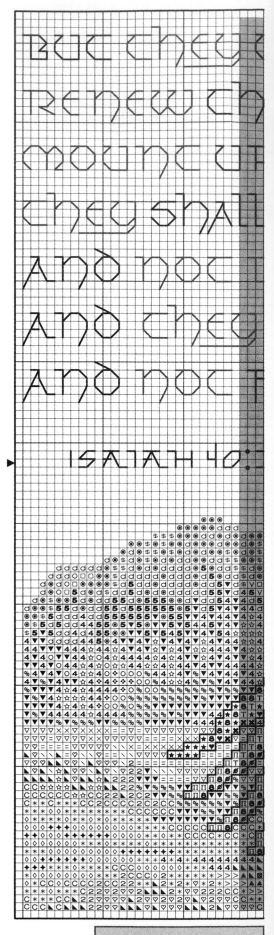

Shaded area indicates last rows stitched on right section.

that wait upon the Lord shall
their strength; they shall
up with wings as eagles;
ll run,
be weary;
y shall walk,
faint.

:31

THE PRAYER OF JABEZ (120 wide x 154 high)

X	DMC	¼X	¾X	B'ST	ANC.	COLOR	X	DMC	¼X	¾X	B'ST	ANC.	COLOR
	155			†		lavender	$	3364				260	lt green
✳[	156					lt blue		3746			□	1030	violet
	* 793			□	176	blue	2	3823			+	386	lt gold
△	158	◢	◹	†		vy dk blue	♦	3828				373	dk gold
♠	327	◤	◺	★	100	dk purple		3828			□	373	dk gold
	327			Υ	100	dk purple	★	3835	◹	◣	★	98	purple
n	341			†	117	lt blue	↑	3836				90	lt purple
◉	407	◥	◹		914	dk flesh		3860			◊	379	taupe
⁘	422				943	gold	8[	3860	◹	◣		379	taupe
⬌	519			+	1038	turquoise		* 3861				378	lt taupe
	792			◊	941	dk blue	✓	3863			Υ	379	brown
¢	827			□	160	lt turquoise		202HL#4			Υ		Kreinik metallic very fine braid
◖	950	◹	◣		4146	flesh		202HL#12			◊		Kreinik metallic tapestry braid
+	951	◸	◪		1010	lt flesh	●	792					dk blue Fr. Knot
□	3042			♡	870	vy lt purple							
♥	3362			+	263	dk green							
◓	3363			◊	262	green							

⬜ Use **1** strand of floss.

* Use **2** strands of first floss color listed and **1** of the second.

† DMC 155 behind hand. DMC 158 for corners. DMC 341 in border.

★ DMC 327 for wording. DMC 3835 for corners.

Υ DMC 327 for wording and small diamonds (**1** strand). Kreinik 202HL #4 Braid for corners (**1** strand). DMC 3863 in border.

+ DMC 519 behind hand. DMC 3823 for sky. DMC 3362 for border.

◊ DMC 792 for wording and behind hand. DMC 3860 for hand (**1** strand). DMC 3363 for border.

□ DMC 827 behind hand. DMC 3746 for corners. DMC 156/793 blend for border (Use **1** strand of each floss color listed).

♡ Kreinik 202HL #12 Braid (**1** strand) couched with **1** strand of 202HL #4 Braid for border around large diamond. DMC 3042 for all other in border.

The Prayer of Jabez was stitched on a 15" x 17" piece of 28 count Tea-dyed Linen (design size 8⅝" x 11") over two fabric threads. Three strands of floss were used for Cross Stitch and 2 strands for French Knots and Backstitch except where noted in color key. It was custom framed.

The Prayer of Jabez (120w x 154h)		
14 count	8⅝"	x 11"
16 count	7½"	x 9⅝"
18 count	6¾"	x 8⅝"

Design by Sandy Orton, Kooler Design Studio.

Photo on page 17

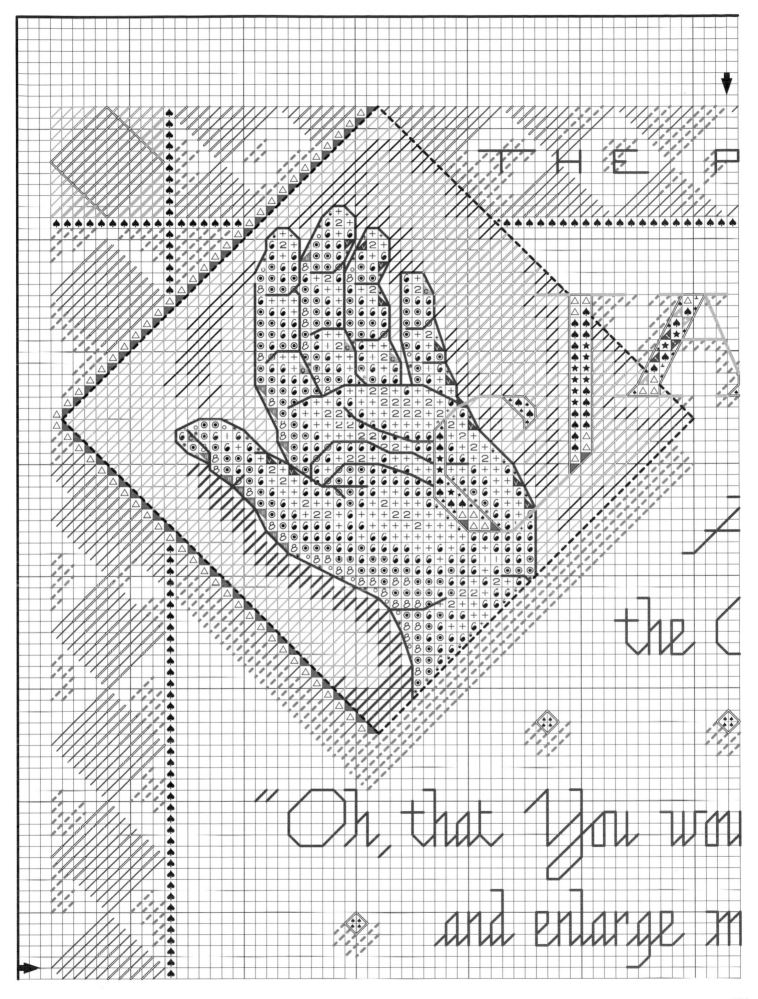

PRAYER OF

JABEZ

And Jabez called on

God of Israel saying,

uld bless me indeed

y territory,

Shaded area indicates last row of previous section of design.

Shaded area indicates last row of previous section of design.

that Your hand wi
and that You would
that I may not
So God grante
reque
I CHRONIC

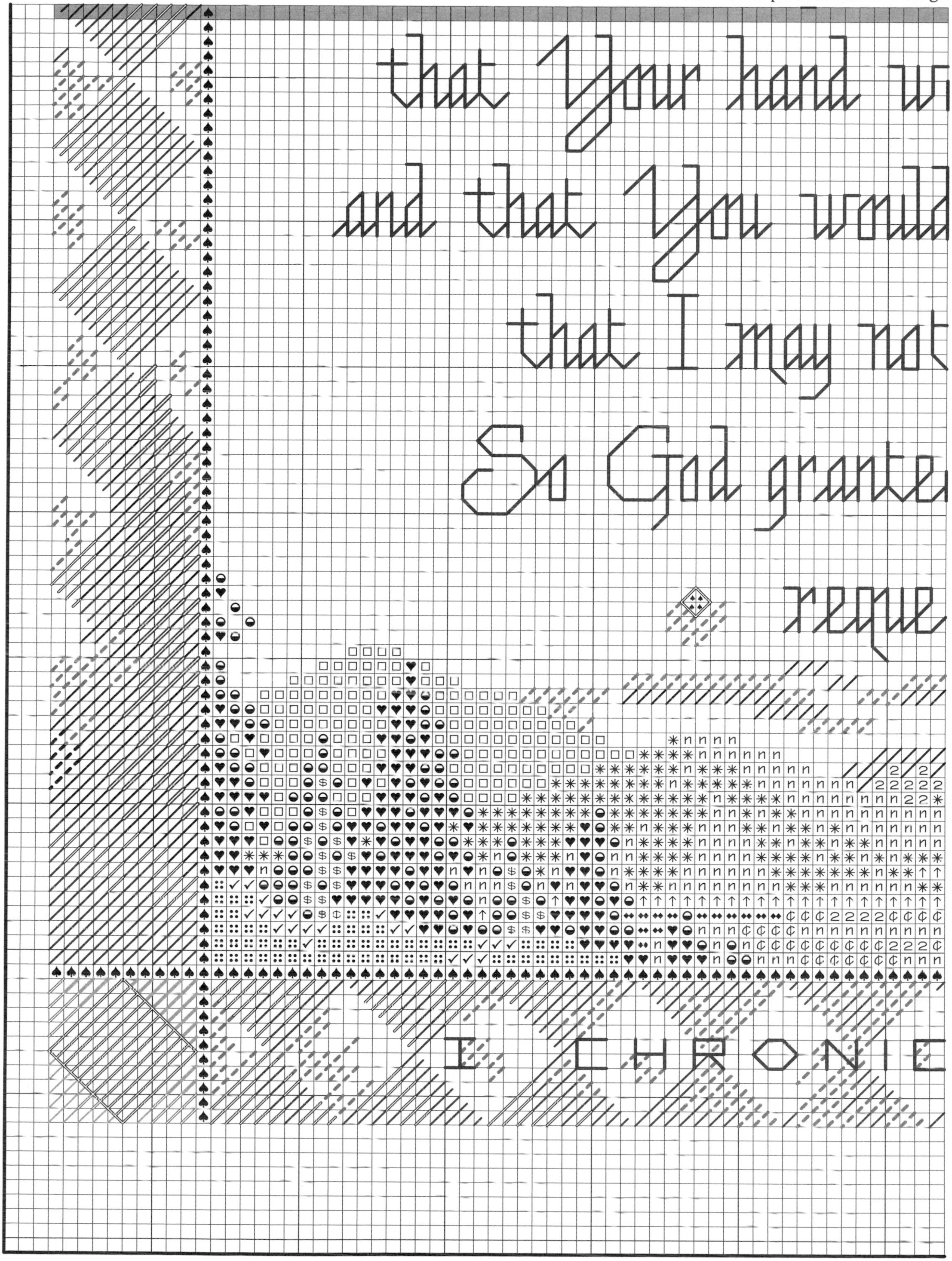

ould be with me

keep me from evil,

cause pain!"

him what he

sted

LES 4:10

Photos on pages 18-19

BOOKMARKS FROM THE PSALMS

1	Stitch Count: 26 wide x 99 high
2	Stitch Count: 26 wide x 100 high
3	Stitch Count: 24 wide x 99 high

Cross Stitch – 2 strands

Symbol	Color	DMC	Anchor
	white	blanc	2
	moss green	320	215
	coral	350	11
	peach	352	9
	dk moss green	367	217
	tan	436	1045
	dk red	498	1005
	bright green	704	256
	bright yellow	726	295
	yellow	743	302
	lt blue	813	161
	red	817	13
	blue	825	162
	dk green	890	218
	green	986	246
	lt green	988	243
	yellow beige	3047	852
	dk yellow green	3346	267
	yellow green	3347	266
	lt yellow green	3348	264
	brown	3371	382
	dk rose	3687	68
	rose	3688	66
	lt rose	3689	49
	fuchsia	3804	63

Backstitch – 1 strand

Symbol	Color
	bright green for #1
	dk green for #2
	green for #3
	blue for wording in #3
	fuchsia for flowers in #1
	brown for "Ps. 17:8" and apple in #3 and
	remaining backstitch in #1 and #2

French Knot – 1 strand

Symbol	Color
	yellow for flower centers in #1
	dk green for #2
	red for buds in #3
	brown for remaining French Knots

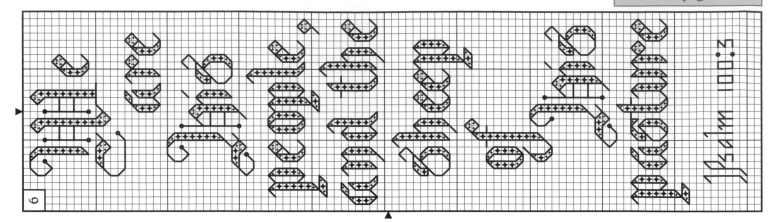

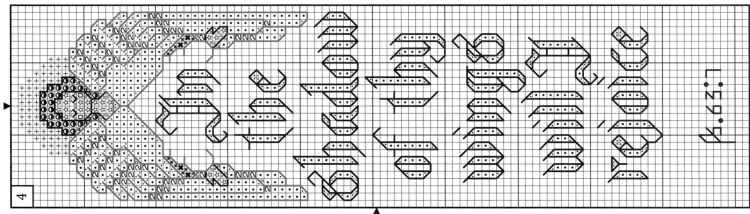

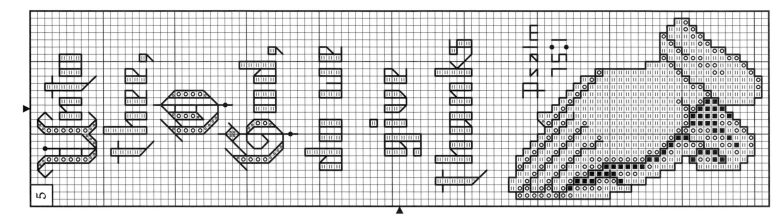

4	Stitch Count: 26 wide x 99 high
5	Stitch Count: 25 wide x 100 high
6	Stitch Count: 26 wide x 99 high

Cross Stitch – 2 strands

Symbol	Color	DMC	Anchor
·	white	blanc	2
	brown	433	358
◐	gold	676	891
+	lt gold	677	886
☆	flesh	754	1012
□	salmon	760	1022
	dk blue	797	132
✦	blue	798	131
	dk brown	898	360
	dk grey blue	930	1035
	grey blue	931	1034
✖	lt grey blue	932	1033
⹀	lt flesh	948	1011
○	dk flesh	950	4146
2	sky blue	3753	1031
■	vy dk flesh	3773	1008

Backstitch – 1 strand

Symbol	Color
╱	dk grey blue
╱	dk blue for #6
╱	dk brown for #5
╱	grey blue for wording in #4
╱	brown for remaining backstitch

French Knot – 1 strand

Symbol	Color
●	dk blue for #6
●	dk brown for #5
●	grey blue for #4

Designs were stitched on white or ecru 18 count bookmarks.

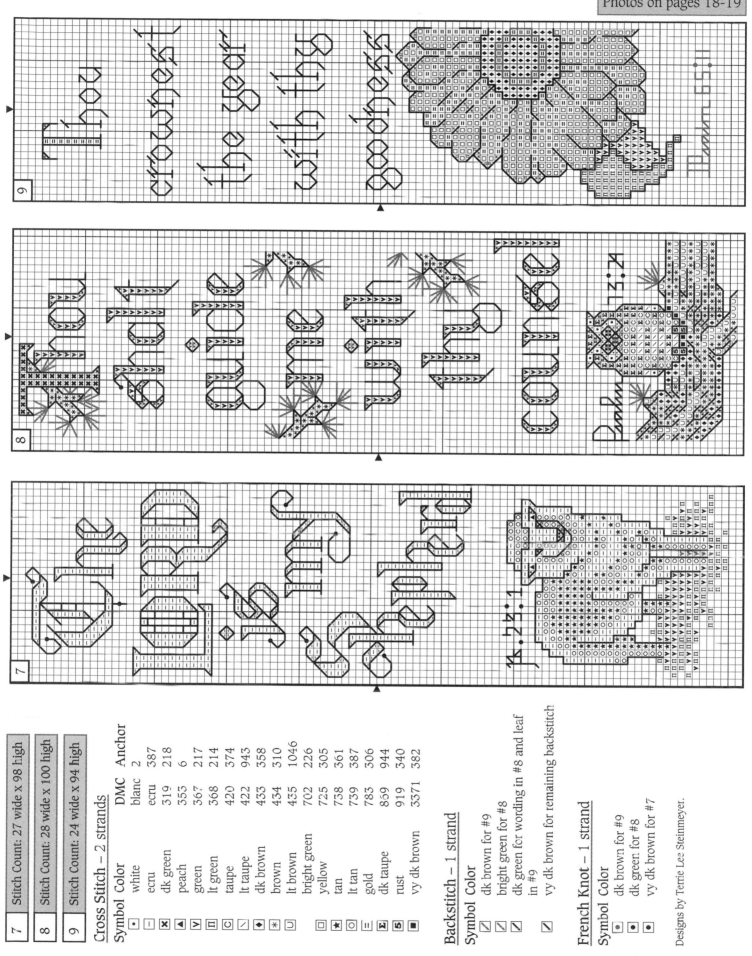

Photos on pages 18-19

7	Stitch Count: 27 wide x 98 high
8	Stitch Count: 28 wide x 100 high
9	Stitch Count: 24 wide x 94 high

Cross Stitch – 2 strands

Symbol	Color	DMC	Anchor
	white	blanc	2
	ecru	ecru	387
	dk green	319	218
	peach	355	6
	green	367	217
	lt green	368	214
	taupe	420	374
	lt taupe	422	943
	dk brown	433	358
	brown	434	310
	lt brown	435	1046
	bright green	702	226
	yellow	725	305
	tan	738	361
	lt tan	739	387
	gold	783	306
	dk taupe	859	944
	rust	919	340
	vy dk brown	3371	382

Backstitch – 1 strand

Symbol	Color
	dk brown for #9
	bright green for #8
	dk green for wording in #8 and leaf in #9
	vy dk brown for remaining backstitch

French Knot – 1 strand

Symbol	Color
	dk brown for #9
	dk green for #8
	vy dk brown for #7

Designs by Terrie Lee Steinmeyer.

BE PRESENT AT OUR TABLE

Stitch Count: 113 wide x 145 high

Project Information: The design was stitched on a 14½" x 16½" piece of 28 count Platinum Cashel Linen over two fabric threads. It was custom framed.

Photo on page 6

Cross Stitch – 3 strands

Symbol	Color	DMC	Anchor
•	blue	930	1035
★	lt blue	3752	1032

Backstitch

Symbol	Color
◰	blue - 2 strands
◰	blue - 1 strand

French Knot & Lazy Daisy

Symbol	Color
•	blue - 2 strands
⊘	blue - 1 strand

Design by Sandy Orton, Kooler Design Studio.

Shaded area indicates first row stitched on bottom section.

THANK YOU FOR THE WORLD

Stitch Count:
89 wide x 118 high

Project Information:
The design was stitched on a 12½" x 14½" piece of 28 count Antique White Cashel Linen over two fabric threads. It was custom framed.

Cross Stitch – 3 strands

Symbol	Color	DMC	Anchor
·	white	blanc	2
✦	mauve	315	1019
▣	grey	318	399
△	periwinkle	340	118

Cross Stitch – 3 strands

Symbol	Color	DMC	Anchor
≡	lt periwinkle	341	117
◆	dk grey	413	236
◇	lt grey	415	398
■	brown	435	1046
◐	lt brown	436	1045
⊠	dk blue	517	162
✦	blue	518	1039
◇	lt blue	519	1038
✳	gold	676	891
‖	tan	738	361
+	yellow	745	300
●	dk beige brown	839	1086
★	beige brown	841	1082

Cross Stitch – 3 strands

Symbol	Color	DMC	Anchor
◙	lt beige brown	842	1080
⊕	dk pink	899	52
-	lt pink	963	73
◀	dk green	987	244
✕	pink	3326	36
◎	green	3347	266
▷	lt green	3348	264
▶	dk periwinkle	3807	122

French Knot & Lazy Daisy – 1 strand

Symbol	Color
●	dk pink
∅	dk pink

Backstitch – 1 strand

Symbol	Color
⧄	dk grey
⧄	mauve for pink flowers, tablecloth, bottom cushion, pink area of bird's chest, and pink icing
⧄	dk blue for blue ribbon, blue bird, flower centers on bonnet, mouse's collar, blue icing, and stripe on apron

Backstitch – 1 strand

Symbol	Color
⧄	dk pink for bows
⧄	dk green for leaves, stems, and green icing
⧄	dk beige brown for remaining backstitch

Design by Sandy Orton, Kooler Design Studio.

Photo on page 6

Shaded area indicates first row stitched on bottom section.

GIVE US GRATEFUL HEARTS

Stitch Count: 74 wide x 116 high

Project Information: The design was stitched on an 11½" x 14½" piece of 28 count Platinum Cashel Linen over two fabric threads. It was custom framed.

Cross Stitch – 3 strands

Symbol	Color	DMC	Anchor
·	white	blanc	2
■	mauve	315	1019
☆	periwinkle	340	118
	dk blue green	501	878
E	blue green	502	877

Cross Stitch – 3 strands

Symbol	Color	DMC	Anchor
◹	yellow	744	301
◣	lt yellow	745	300
◉	salmon	760	1022
□	lt salmon	761	1021
▶	blue	794	175
○	violet	3041	871
◿	lt violet	3042	870
◆	lt green	3348	264
	pink	3688	66
✕	lt blue	3747	120
	dk periwinkle	3807	122

Backstitch – 1 strand

Symbol	Color
◿	white
◿	mauve for roses and ribbons
◿	dk blue green for leaves and stems
◿	dk periwinkle for wording, birds, and hearts

French Knot – 1 strand

Symbol	Color
●	white
●	dk periwinkle

Photo on page 6

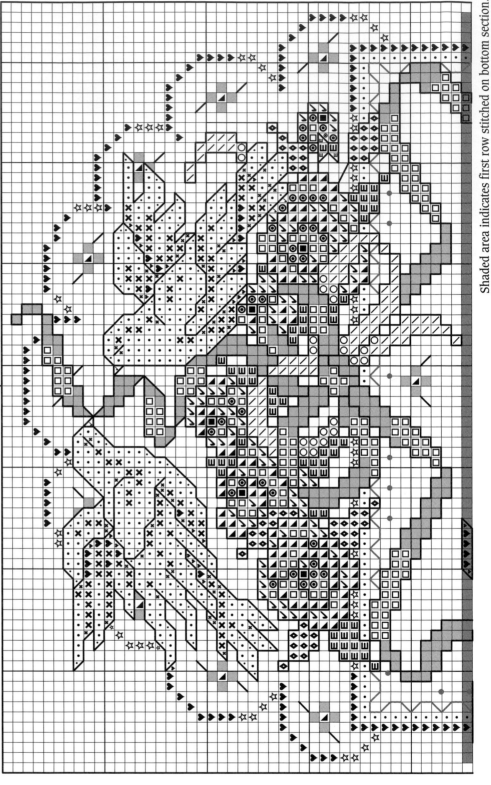

Design by Sandy Orton, Kooler Design Studio.

Shaded area indicates first row stitched on bottom section.

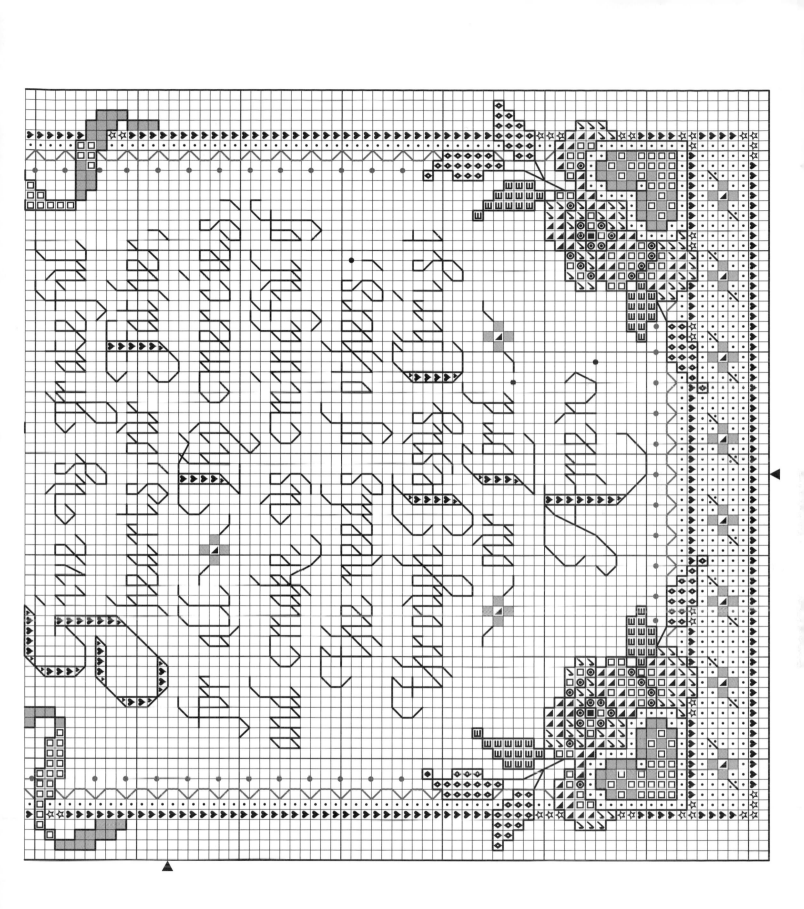

BLESS, O LORD

Stitch Count:
89 wide x 75 high

Project Information: The design was stitched on a 12½" x 11½" piece of 28 count Antique White Cashel Linen over two fabric threads. It was custom framed.

Cross Stitch – 3 strands

Symbol	Color	DMC	Anchor
⊡	white	blanc	2
▽	lt lavender	209	109
■	black	310	403
	purple	333	119
	grey	414	235
◆	brown	434	310
⊡	lt brown	435	1046
◎	lavender	553	98
▼	dk blue green	561	212
⊙	blue green	562	210

Cross Stitch – 3 strands

Symbol	Color	DMC	Anchor
⊙	lt blue green	563	208
⊠	pink	604	55
△	lt pink	605	1094
⊟	gold	676	891
⊞	lt gold	677	886
✳	yellow	725	305
⊟	lt yellow	727	293
⊕	dk gold	729	890
⧯	lt grey	762	234
✦	blue	813	161
◇	lt blue	827	160
⊠	dk brown	898	360
⊕	green	988	243
▲	dk green	3345	268
✕	lt green	3348	264
☆	lt mauve	3687	68
▢	mauve	3803	972
▽	violet	3807	122

Backstitch – 1 strand

Symbol	Color
∕	dk blue green
∕	black for bees
∕	grey for bee trails
∕	dk brown for hive
∕	mauve for pink flowers
∕	violet for wording
∕	purple for remaining backstitch

French Knot & Lazy Daisy– 1 strand

Symbol	Color
◉	black for bees
◉	yellow for blue flowers
⊙	violet
⊘	black

Design by Sandy Orton, Kooler Design Studio.

Photo on page 6

PATRIOTIC HOLIDAYS

Stitch Count: 65 wide x 74 high

Project Information: The design was stitched on an 11" x 11½" piece of 14 count Antique White Aida. It was custom framed.

Cross Stitch – 3 strands

Symbol	Color	DMC	Anchor
•	white	blanc	2
▣	grey	317	400
✦	dk red	498	1005

Cross Stitch – 3 strands

Symbol	Color	DMC	Anchor
V	red	666	46
✎	yellow	743	302
△	lt yellow	746	275
−	lt grey	762	234
✳	blue	798	131
♥	dk brown	839	1086
✔	brown	840	1084
○	lt blue	3325	129

Design by Linda Gillum, Kooler Design Studio.

Backstitch – 1 strand

Symbol	Color
╱	grey for stars, claws, flags, and poles
╱	blue for Scripture, Reference, and border
╱	dk brown for eagle's beak and body

French Knot – 1 strand

Symbol	Color
◉	white

Photo on page 27

SPEAKING OF ANGELS

Stitch Count: 108 wide x 348 high

Project Information: The design was stitched on a 14" x 31" piece of 28 count Cream Cashel Linen over two fabric threads. It was custom framed.

Cross Stitch – 3 strands

Symbol	Color	DMC	Anchor
❖	ecru	ecru	387
⊟	vy dk pink	221	897
◪	rust	356	5975
	yellow beige	371	854
◩ *	dk brown & lt brown	433 & 435	358 & 1046
	dk brown	433	358
✪	brown	434	310
◖	lt brown	435	1046
☐	vy lt brown	436	1045
◿	tan	437	362
✚ †	lt gold & gold metallic	729 & 002HL	890
	lt gold	729	890
➤	lt tan	738	361
◨	flesh	758	868
■	lt pink	760	1022
◗	vy dk brown	801	359
▷	coffee brown	838	1088
✦	dk blue	924	851
✳ *	lt blue & vy lt blue	926 & 927	850 & 848
	lt blue	926	850
·	vy lt blue	927	848
⊓	lt flesh	945	881
◐	vy lt flesh	951	1010
☆	dk coffee brown	3021	905
	grey	3023	1040
	lt grey	3024	397
$	lt yellow beige	3046	887
8	dk flesh	3064	883
◤	pink	3712	1023
◣	dk pink	3721	896
◪	blue	3768	779
◺	vy dk flesh	3772	1007
	gold metallic	002HL	

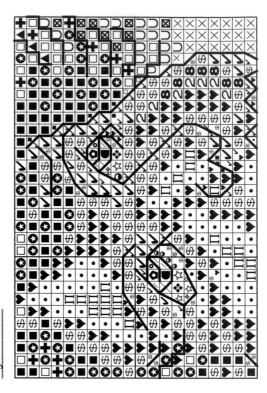

Half Cross Stitch – 1 strand

Symbol	Color	DMC	Anchor
⊠	yellow beige	371	854
●	lt blue	926	850
◀	vy lt blue	927	848
⊔	lt yellow beige	3046	887
⊠	blue	3768	779

Backstitch – 1 strand

⬩	vy dk pink for upper lip and pink portion of wing
⬩	coffee brown for cherub and wing
⬩	dk coffee brown for lettering

French Knot – 1 strand

●	dk coffee brown

* 2 strands of first color, 1 strand of second

† 2 strands of first color, 1 strand of Kreinik Blending Filament #002HL

Needlework adaptation by Sandy Orton, Kooler Design Studio and Linda Culp Calhoun.

Eye Detail

Photo on page 20

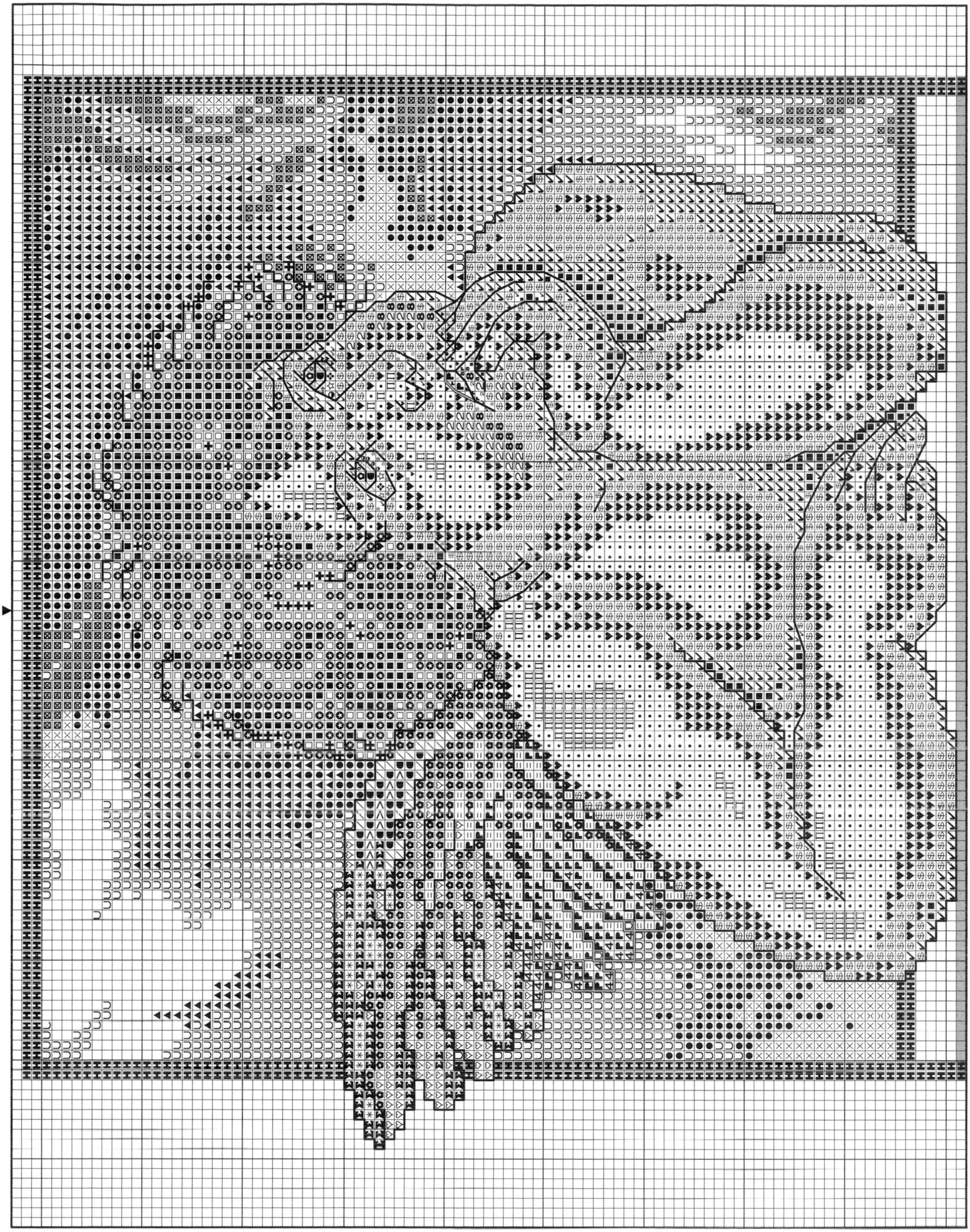

Shaded area indicates 1 row overlap.

For He will give His angels charge concerning
you, to guard you in all your ways. They will
bear you up in their hands, lest you strike
your foot against a stone. Ps. 91:11-12

They are like angels and are sons of God,
Luke 20:36 ... Be not forgetful to entertain
strangers: for thereby some have entertained
angels unawares. Heb. 13:2 ... And the angel
said to them, "Behold, I bring you good news
of a great joy which shall be to all the people;
for today in the city of David there has been
born for you a Savior, who is Christ the
Lord. Luke 2:10-11 ... And the angel of His

Shaded area indicates 1 row overlap.

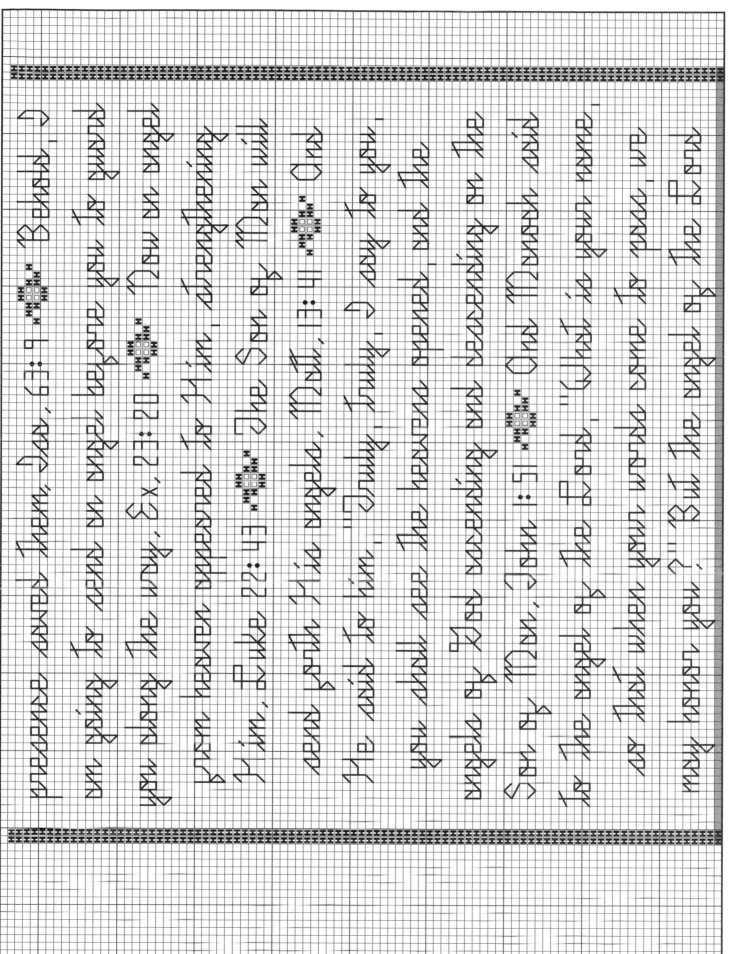

Shaded area indicates 1 row overlap.

...and to him, "Why do you ask my name, seeing...

I give you thanks, O Lord, with my whole heart; ... Judges 13:17,18

before the angels I sing your praise. Ps. 138:1

Open this ... and ... angels standing ...

The four corners of the earth, holding the four winds ... Rev. 7:1

... His angels, mighty in strength, ... Bless ...

The Lord ... His angels ... His word, ... Ps. 103:20

... who perform His word, ... Cherish ...

... joy in the presence of the angels ... Luke 15:10

94

stitcher's guide

COLOR KEYS AND CHARTS

Each chart is made up of a key and a gridded design where each square represents a stitch. The symbols in the key tell which floss color to use for each stitch in the chart.

Quarter Stitches and Three-Quarter Stitches are used occasionally for fine details. The color key will indicate which reduced symbols are for these stitches.

STITCHES

Beginning and Ending Stitches — When beginning or ending a length of floss, always secure the floss end under stitches; never tie knots. At the beginning of a row of cross stitches, leave a tail of floss on the back of fabric and stitch over it with the first few cross stitches. This will secure the end. When ending a length of floss, run the floss under several stitches on the back of fabric to secure (*Diagram A*).

Diagram A

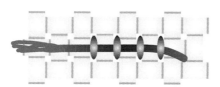

Cross Stitch — When working stitches in a horizontal row, follow numbers in *Diagram B* to work stitches from left to right and then back again. When working stitches vertically, follow numbers in *Diagram C* to complete each stitch before you move down to work the next stitch. When working stitches over two fabric threads on linen or similar fabrics, follow numbers in *Diagram D*.

Diagram B

Diagram C

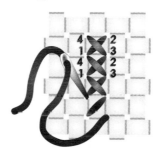

Diagram D

Quarter Stitch — Work one-quarter of a Cross Stitch, splitting the fabric threads when working on Aida (*Diagram E*) or only crossing one thread when working over two threads on linen or similar fabrics (*Diagram F*).

Diagram E

Diagram F

Three-Quarter Stitch — Work three-quarters of a Cross Stitch by following numbers in *Diagram G* when working on Aida. When working stitches over two fabric threads on linen or similar fabrics, follow numbers in *Diagram H*.

Continued on page 96.

Diagram G

Diagram H

Diagram M

Half Cross Stitch — Follow numbers in *Diagram I* to work stitches from left to right on Aida. Follow numbers in *Diagram J* when working over two threads on linen or similar fabrics.

Lazy Daisy Stitch — Follow numbers in *Diagram N* to bring needle up at 1 and form a loop. Take needle down at 1 and up at 2, catching the loop under the tip of the needle. Pull needle through fabric and go down at 2 on other side of loop.

Diagram I

Diagram J

Diagram N

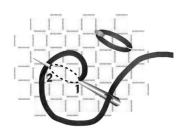

Backstitch — Work backstitching after all cross stitching is completed. Follow numbers in *Diagram K* when working Backstitch on Aida. Follow numbers in *Diagram L* when working over two threads on linen or similar fabrics.

Beads — Add beads after all cross stitching is completed. Follow numbers in *Diagram O* to bring needle up at 1. Run the floss through the bead and take needle down at 2. When working over two threads on linen or similar fabrics, follow numbers in *Diagram P*.

Diagram K

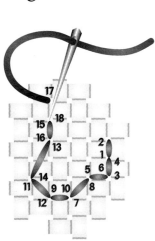

Diagram L

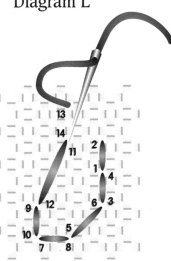

Diagram O

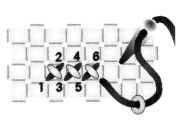

Diagram P

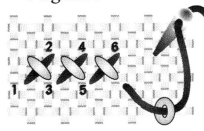

Couching — Following numbers in *Diagram Q*, use 1 strand of tapestry braid for long stitch and 1 strand of very fine braid for tie-down stitches.

Diagram Q

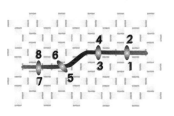

French Knot — Follow numbers in *Diagram M* to bring needle up at 1. Wind floss once around needle and take needle down at 2, holding loose end of floss tight until knot is formed.